Guiltless Living

Guiltless Living

Confessions of a Serial Sinner

Captured by the Grace of God

GINGER HUBBARD

Shepherd Press
Wapwallopen, Pennsylvania

Trade Paperback ISBN: 978-1-936908639
eBook ISBN
Mobi format: ISBN 978-1-936908-653
ePub format: ISBN 978-1-936908-646

Published by Shepherd Press
P.O. Box 24
Wapwallopen, Pennsylvania 18660

Page design and typesetting by Lakeside Design Plus
Cover design by Tobias' Outerwear for Books
First Printing, 2014
Printed in the United States of America

BP 23 22 21 20 19 18 17 16 15 14 13
14 13 12 11 10 9 8 7 6 5 4 3 2 1

Library of Congress Control Number: 2014931613
eBook information: Go to: http://www.shepherdpress.com/ebooks

Contents

Acknowledgments

With all my heart, I'd like to thank:

My husband and my best friend, Ronnie. In January of 2009, I shelved this finished manuscript and, with a broken heart, believed I would never write again. Thank you for motivating me to pull it back out, blow off the dust and refresh it with all the good God has done. You are my rainbow after the storm. I love you with every ounce of my being.

My incredible children—excuse me, *teenagers*—Wesley and Alex. Your encouragement and support spurred me on more than you will ever know. Not once did you complain about the time I spent writing this book. Thank you for your unselfish support and desire for others to know Jesus through my writing.

My faithful friend, Al Roland. The time you spend praying for and serving Preparing the Way Ministries in many capacities will surely earn you an enormous, shining jewel on your crown. You are always one click away from lending a helping hand and you are readily available to answer my random and sometimes off-the-wall questions, like "What are those stripe thingies in the middle of the road called?" or "How do you spell *déjà vu*?" I also appreciate the verses you found and insights offered. You are a tremendous help and blessing in so many ways.

Deborah Stabler. You probably had the toughest job of all, ironing out the wrinkles of my first draft. Thanks for your hard work and dedication.

Irene Stoops. I appreciate your honesty in challenging me to rewrite a section in the miserly chapter. Your wisdom, insights, and careful editing certainly made this a better book.

Sue Lutz. What I admire and appreciate most about your editing (and your heart) is your dedication to a Christ-centered, gospel focus. You brought to my attention the areas where my practicality weakened that focus and you challenged me to hold true to the heart of the gospel. Thank you for polishing the apple with your strong editorial talents.

Bart Lipscomb. The time you spent researching biblical references for every chapter was extremely helpful. May your wisdom and zeal for God's Word always bring him glory!

Pre-publication readers. Many thanks to all of you who read through the manuscript and offered helpful suggestions: Chuck and Bonnie Ferrell, Wesley Ferrell, Steven and Gina Ferrell, Toma Knight, Rebecca Ingram Powell, Marlo Francis, Lisa O'Quinn, Christy Truitt, Merrilyn (MiMi) Henry, Candy Prater, Linda Currie, Carl Ettinger, Cierra Cooke, Peggy Slocumb, Linda Drummond, Cindy Thrash, Beth Walton, Faye Kirk, Michelle Hunt, Rhonda Boothe, Brandi Streetman, and Melissa Gatlin.

My friends at Shepherd Press. I count it a great privilege and blessing to be part of such a Christ-centered publishing house. There are so many writers with far more wisdom and talent, yet you continue to print my books. It's a mystery I do not take for granted. I am forever grateful for your support and confidence in me.

My Savior and Lord, Jesus Christ. Thank you for loving and saving this serial sinner. May these pages bring you glory.

Christ Jesus came into the world to save sinners
—of whom I am the worst.

1 Timothy 1:15

Introduction

The Bible teaches us to "confess your sins to each other" (James 5:16). I believe that when we are willing to be open and honest about our own struggles, God uses that openness to encourage others to do the same. In writing for several national publications, I am often attacked for my transparency. It never fails. Anytime I acknowledge the wickedness of my heart by revealing a sinful attitude or action that brought God's conviction, I receive many condemning emails. Statements such as, "I can't believe you call yourself a Christian!" and "You are an evil wolf in sheep's clothing!" fill my inbox.

Throughout this book you may find some of the things I reveal about myself shocking. There will be some who conclude, "This woman is horrible! She has no business writing a book or teaching the Word of God." You may be tempted to send me a letter telling me what a wicked sinner I am. Please, if you have that temptation, I hope you save your paper and ink or your fingertips. I know I am a sinner. I am fully aware of how wicked my heart can be. As a matter of fact, if the apostle Paul were alive today, I would challenge him for ownership of his words, "Christ died for sinners—of whom I am the worst."

In reading some of my confessions, you may find me unlikable at times. But I will not sugarcoat the wickedness of my heart. When sin rears its head, there is nothing likable about it. It's ugly, dark, shocking, and offensive, especially when we are willing to search our hearts and be fully honest about what is there. I hope that an honest, transparent revelation of what sin looks like will provoke deep thought and self-evaluation in the hearts of my readers. The Bible states, "Whoever conceals their sins does not prosper, but the one who confesses and renounces them finds mercy" (Prov. 28:13).

There are dangers I risk in sharing my confessions. While I may fail in my attempt to avoid these dangers, I want you to at least understand my motive. Sometimes, when we step back and look at our behavior, we find it so ridiculous that it becomes humorous. But let me clarify one thing here. Sin is not a laughing matter. The things that God sent his Son to die for are not funny. However, I see nothing wrong with laughing at ourselves and how ridiculously we behave at times. My motive is not to make light of sin, but to acknowledge how utterly foolish I can be when I am living out of my sinful nature rather than in Christ. Once I have repented, I often find myself shaking my head with a dumbfounded grin on my face as I look back on my own foolishness and say to my Savior, "Lord, how ridiculous I would be apart from you!"

Another risk I run in sharing examples of my foolishness is giving the impression that I am boasting in sin. It bothers me to hear a testimony where the Christian spends more time detailing his colorful past than what Jesus has done to restore and redeem him. Please know that I am opening the dark chapters of my heart only to offer a greater appreciation for the Book of Life, which tells of the glorious grace of God toward repentant sinners. I do not wish to boast in sin, but in the great things God has done and continues to do in my life, in hopes that you might open yourself up for the same.

Some of you will relate to my transparency. You desire the Holy Spirit to search your heart for hidden sin and you welcome any avenue for God's work to be done in your life. Others will find my confessions offensive and will harbor an attitude of condemnation toward me. I do not say this to be harsh, just as I do not wave my dirty laundry to be offensive or to merely satisfy curious minds as to the depths of my sins. I confess in hopes that it will encourage you to search your own heart. Through searching comes revelation, which leads to confession, which leads to repentance, which leads to forgiveness, which leads to sanctification, which leads to a deeper, more real relationship with God.

Without acknowledgment of sin, there can be no repentance or forgiveness. In other words, if we are not being "real," the work of God's Spirit within us is hindered. Shallow confessions result in a shallow work of the Spirit. It's when we are willing to hand over hidden sins, the ones we would rather not admit are buried in our hearts, that we drink deeply from the living waters of God's goodness and grace. That's my desire for you. The Bible says, "The purposes of a person's heart are deep waters, but one who has insight draws them out" (Prov. 20:5).

Please know that my aim is for us all to grow closer to Jesus. I humbly challenge you to consider your reaction to the shocking truths of my heart. As you do, ask yourself two questions: Am I willing to acknowledge my own sinful capabilities? Do I extend God's grace to sinners through my attitudes and actions toward them?

We cannot fully appreciate the depths of God's holiness until we fully acknowledge the depths of our sinfulness. It is for this reason that God calls Christians to be real. The sooner we face the reality of our depravity, the sooner we accept God's atonement for that depravity and enter into the freedom of *guiltless living*.

The Critical Serial Sinner

and the Encouraging Grace of God

My friend Marlo and I led a "Girls at Heart" conference together in a state I will not name. We found out that we are like oil and water when it comes to our responses to tough situations. Marlo goes with the flow, looks at the positive side of things, and remains cheerful in the midst of not-so-ideal circumstances. Me? Let's just say I don't.

I was critical of the town the minute we stepped off the plane. It was my first visit to this particular state and I was not impressed. I have encountered chicken houses, paper mills, and pastures before, but nothing compared to the foul odor of this town. It followed us from the airport to the restaurant we dined in, to the church, and to the hotel. It was like being caged in an inescapable stink prison. We were told that the odor was from the manure used to fertilize the fields—all fifty bazillion acres of them. My hair stank, my clothes stank, and even the pillow I brought from home seemed to absorb the smell. It was nauseating.

During the three-hour drive from the airport to the town where we were to speak, we reacted like polar opposites. Marlo had her head sticking out the window like a cocker spaniel puppy taking in the scenery, while I had one hand on the steering wheel and the other covering my nose and mouth. "How could you possibly be enjoying this?" I whined through a pinched nasal passage. "It's like a doo-doo bomb exploded! This is so nasty! Get your head back in the car so I can roll up the windows!" Always the encourager, Marlo replied, "Oh, it's not that bad! We'll get used to it. Have you ever seen so many pastures? What beautiful land! And just look at those storybook farmhouses! This is amazing!"

Amazingly stinky, I thought.

The conference went well, but I never got used to the foul odor. I was more than ready to say my goodbyes, leave the kind people to their stinky state, and hightail it back to Alabama. On the return drive to the airport, we discovered that I had made a mistake in coordinating our flight departure times. While Marlo would arrive in plenty of time to make her flight, my flight was scheduled to leave in two hours. We were still two hours shy of reaching the airport. I panicked, stomped the accelerator pedal, and started complaining about how far we had to drive from Smellville to the airport. "I'll never make it in time," I complained. "They should have flown us into a closer airport so we didn't have to drive so far. And if they had any consideration at all, the least they could have done is provide us with gas masks!"

To make matters worse, the rental car was running on empty. I hadn't noticed that we were low on gas until the warning signal beeped. "We haven't passed an exit in miles, so surely one is coming up," Marlo chirped. No such luck. There we were, two southern belles, out in the middle of nowhere, about to run out of gas. Pasture after pasture whizzed by for many miles, but no exits. The needle on the fuel gauge pointed below empty. Just when I was about to go on a rampage, drunk from panic, impatience, and toxic cow patty fumes, an exit appeared over the horizon like a mirage. My breathing steadied and hope rose in my chest. However, at the end of the exit ramp, we found no gas stations, no stores, no phones—nothing. There were only more pastures and more stink. Correction: there was one house, but believe me when I say that no one in her right mind would have approached it. We're talking *Silence of the Lambs.* We felt confident that if we were to knock on the door, one or both of us would wind up in someone's freezer.

Sweet, patient, positive Marlo set to praying. "Dear Lord, we know that you are with us. We are really frightened and desperate. Please give us direction and lead us to safety." She was a picture of faith. Ginger the critic yelled, "This is the stupidest thing I've ever seen! Why have an exit that leads to nothing? No gas! No phones! No civilization! What's the matter with these people? Who would live here? There's something seriously wrong with this town, Marlo! I mean, where do they buy gas, and groceries, and clothes? This isn't a town; it's the *Twilight Zone*! What are we going to do? Our cells have no signal, and there's no one around for miles. We're going to die in this God-forsaken, rancid place!"

After ten more miles, we finally entered a town. It reminded me of the deserted ghost towns featured in old Westerns. A tumbleweed rolled by. We spotted a parking lot full of cars in front of a school. It was Sunday morning, so we assumed the school was being used as a church, which would explain the full parking lot. Hoping someone could direct us to a gas station, I wheeled up beside the double doors and bolted out of the car in search of a rescuer. Much to my surprise and disappointment, the doors were locked with chains, and the milky windows revealed an empty building. It was at this point that I completely lost it. "Where is everyone, Marlo?" I exploded. "This is the most insane day of my life! This nightmare is never going to end! We're trapped in an Alfred Hitchcock movie and I'm not even wearing clean underwear! We'll never make it to a gas station!" Desperate and very close to tears, I plopped down into the car and pounded the steering wheel, while Marlo gently reminded, "God is in control. He will see us through this."

We spotted a lady sporting a robe and pink fuzzy slippers walking her dog. When we inquired about gas, she scratched her head as if we had all the time in the world and replied, "Gas, you say? Don't reckon we got no gas stations 'round here. You gone have to take to the highway for oh, say twenty miles or so, 'fore you come up on a gas station." At this point, I was catatonic, so Marlo took over the conversation. "Surely you know someone who has some gas close by?" Marlo smiled. More scratching of the head. "Well, I think Herman keeps some gas at his place. You can probably find Herman over at Joe's bar, two blocks down and on the left." We thanked the lady and set off to find Herman, both of us thinking the same thing: *A bar at ten o'clock on Sunday morning . . . um . . . okay.*

Herman was like an angel in overalls. He left his stool in Joe's, had us follow him to his place, and filled our tank to full. I actually made my flight three minutes before they closed the gate. However, I can't say that I got an "A" for attitude.

Critical Serial Sinner: A fault-finding destroyer of good who chooses to search for bad in people or situations, compulsively voices negativity, and lives in bondage to an ungrateful heart.

The Encouraging Grace of God

In some ways, Jesus encountered a similar situation with the woman at the well. However, he handled it much differently. Jews considered Samaria a "stinky" state. The thought of being contaminated typically kept the Jews away, but Jesus purposely went there. Upon arrival Jesus was tired from the day, but rather than criticizing the town and its occupants, he offered the woman at the well the gift of God's living water (John 4:10). When her initial response was to throw the gift back in his face and basically accuse him of thinking he was better than everybody else, Jesus didn't retaliate with justified criticism. He didn't throw her down the well and walk off mumbling about what he did and did not deserve. What he did do was patiently explain, "Everyone who drinks this water [well water] will be thirsty again, but whoever drinks the water I give them will never thirst. Indeed, the water I give them will become in them a spring of water welling up to eternal life" (John 4:13-14).

Jesus didn't enter the stinky state looking to get his tank filled the way I did. He went to fill the tank of another. Interestingly, the first thing he asked the woman for was a drink of water. I find it curious that there is no record that Jesus ever got any. He wanted water, he asked for water, but he wound up putting his needs aside to encourage and fill the needs of another. In fact, the woman wound up testifying to the ways in which Jesus encouraged her, and as a result many believed in him (John 4:39). That's a far cry from how I handled things in the stinky state. I went seeking to get my own tank filled without a single thought of filling someone else's. Oh, the differences between a serial sinner and the Savior of the world! I pray that next time I'll be more like him in my responses.

Jesus walked all the way to a different town—he didn't own a Chevy Tahoe—to encourage others. I have been guilty of avoiding eye contact with someone I recognize in the grocery store in order to guard my time. The comparison sends a shiver of conviction down my spine. How many times could I have taken a moment to speak kind words to a friend who may have been in desperate need of encouragement? How many opportunities were snuffed out by my selfishness? How many times did a critical attitude toward a situation keep me from ministering to someone in need? It's scary to think about.

We may attempt to excuse our critical attitudes by saying Jesus didn't face the same situations and temptations that we face. Life is busier today. He had more time to be an encourager than we do. Not true. It is written in Hebrews, "For we do not have a high priest who is unable to empathize with our weaknesses, but we have one who has been tempted in every way, just as we are—yet he was without sin" (4:15). Jesus encountered every temptation. He endured trying days, tough situations, hard-headed people, blatant offenses, and personal attacks, each time setting an example that we might follow.

However, Jesus also knew we would fall short. Because we are serial sinners, we will not always put others first. We can thank God that he has already atoned for the sins of selfishness and critical attitudes. When we blow it, we can seek forgiveness and begin again. Because of Jesus' work at Calvary, we do not have to live in constant guilt when we mess up. We can receive his forgiveness, accept his atonement, and move forward in his grace.

Zacchaeus was a chief tax collector, reviled as a sinner and overall "bad guy" by the local townspeople (Luke 19:1-9). I picture him as a balding little man with sweaty palms and a shady shrewdness. Think of the character Mr. Potter in It's a Wonderful Life. He was a man who seemed worthy of criticism, but rather than criticizing Zacchaeus's bad points as the others did, Jesus befriended and encouraged him. He could have taken small jabs and gotten a chuckle out of the others. He could have yelled up to the top of the sycamore tree, "Hey, Shortstop! Come on down here and I'll let you chat with me." Instead, he encouraged Zacchaeus by choosing to visit his home. Jesus singled him out from all the people standing around, the man least likely to be chosen. Jesus astonished everyone by honoring the least honorable man there. As a result, Zacchaeus's heart was changed forever through the power of loving encouragement.

Matthew 8 records Jesus healing a man with leprosy. I imagine that the man looked pretty bad, yet Jesus made no critical remark about his appearance. He saw only the man's heart, and he went after it. He encouraged the man through touch and healed him both physically and spiritually. Many people are encouraged through touch. I love for someone to touch my arm in greeting or to hug me as I'm leaving. I feel encouraged when my husband puts his arm around me or a friend pats my back. I remember an instance when I was upset about something and my friend Lisa kissed my hand, with her compassion overflowing. It was a radical show of love and encouraged me so deeply that I will never forget it.

During Jesus' time on earth, he was never given to criticism, even when he was sinned against. Sometimes, even after we forgive, we want to "discuss" the issue, which typically involves dragging someone else through the mud of condemnation. There have been times when I have forgiven my husband for something but then wanted to talk through the details of the offense, often more than once. Jesus didn't do that. He didn't hash over every detail of what people did wrong. He encouraged them, not only through forgiveness, but also through the mercy of not raking them over the coals in a critical fashion. For example, when Jesus forgave the woman caught in adultery, he didn't even mention the outward sin she had committed. He covered it with forgiveness and encouraged her with simple words, "Go now and leave your life of sin" (John 8:11).

Jesus always followed forgiveness with encouragement. His forgiveness and encouragement were exemplified in the life of the father who welcomed home his prodigal son without criticism. The father may have been tempted to say to his repentant boy, "Son, I forgive you, but I do want to talk about what you did with all that money. How much of it was spent on wine? How much was spent on women? Let's discuss why what you did was wrong and how deeply it hurt your mother and me." The father recognized the important thing: the young man was broken and repentant. The son returned whole-heartedly to his father, and that outweighed everything he did before. The father made a choice to encourage rather than criticize. And it was a choice that honored God, blessed his son, and bore witness to the power of the gospel.

Jesus set the example of looking at all situations from an eternal perspective. When we view every situation through the lens of the gospel, we see God's goodness. There is a great theological debate over who causes what. I won't get into it because I am no theologian. However, humans by nature have a tendency to spiritually judge situations according to the way they feel to us. If something feels bad, we tend to adopt a critical attitude and point fingers at Satan. If something feels good, we praise God for the great thing he has done. Rather than arguing over who caused what to happen, it is better to focus on which perspective or lens we will view it through—the eternal or the temporal. Through the eternal lens we are reminded that "in all things [good and bad] God works for the good of those who love him, who have been called according to his purpose" (Rom. 8:28).

I'm not saying that there isn't a Devil or that sickness is not the result of the fall of man. I am saying that if we only perceive bad situations as the work of Satan or blame them on someone else, we develop a critical attitude and miss what God has for us. God desires us to get beyond the way a situation looks or feels and live in the hope that he is in control of all things. In believing this, we are able to "give thanks in all circumstances, for this is God's will for [us] in Christ Jesus" (1 Thess. 5:18).

Joseph was a man whose life reflected the example of Christ, though he lived many centuries earlier. In recalling a negative situation, he exhibited his faith in God through the words he said to his brothers: "You intended to harm me, but God intended it for good . . ." (Gen. 50:20). Joseph trusted that God was in control of even the worst situations. Therefore, he praised God rather than criticizing his brothers for the hardships he had suffered. When we are willing to trust God even in bad situations, critical thinking melts away and we begin to respond as Jesus responded to his upcoming encounter with evil in the garden of Gethsemane: "Shall I not drink the cup the Father has given me?" (John 18:11). The cup the *Father* has given me. Facing death by crucifixion would certainly qualify as the worst of situations. Yet Jesus didn't ask, "Why me?" He didn't criticize those involved with the evil done against him. He knew that the Father's plan served a much higher purpose than the temporal situation.

Jesus never criticized or complained, always encouraged, and always exemplified what it means to trust the Father in all things. Through the indwelling power of the Holy Spirit, God enables his children to do the same. And when his children disregard the power of the Holy Spirit and fall into critical thinking and behavior, he graciously atones for their sins. What a good God we serve!

God Calls Christians to Encourage

Throughout Scripture, God commands us to encourage one another. In Hebrews we are told to "consider how we may spur one another on toward love and good deeds" (10:24), and in 1 Thessalonians we are instructed to "encourage one another and build each other up" (5:11). As I studied these verses, one word suddenly jumped off the page with deeper meaning. I became intrigued with the word "consider." We are to "*consider* how we may spur one another on toward love and good deeds." According to Webster's Dictionary, *consider* means to "think about seriously; to take into account; to show consideration for; to regard highly."[1] In specifically applying these definitions to the context of speaking encouragement into the lives of others, we must think seriously before we speak; take into account how our words might be perceived before they are spoken; show consideration for the feelings, circumstances, and best interests of the one who will receive the words; and regard highly (above ourselves) the person to whom the words are directed (Phil. 2:3).

Consideration takes time but it prevents critical words from being spoken. Solomon puts it more fluently. "The heart of the righteous weighs its answers, but the mouth of the wicked gushes evil" (Prov. 15:28). Consideration is not done off the cuff. It's not speaking the first thing that pops into our heads. It's not blurting out words under the influence of anger, impatience or frustration. It's taming the tongue to restrain itself and yield to careful consideration before wagging, lest we discourage others and receive an SUI (Speaking Under the Influence) citation from the Holy Spirit.

Let's continue the story we started at the beginning of the chapter. Upon my return to the Atlanta airport from Smellville, I was still faced with a ninety-minute drive home. Marlo had flown back to her home state, so I was traveling the last stretch alone. It was late and I was cranky. The two vanilla lattes with extra cream were putting on the pressure. The sign read ten miles to the next exit. *Déjà vu* set in. *Twilight Zone* music came out of nowhere. Was the saga to continue? The lattes were screaming for release so, as Sally Field so eloquently put it in *Smokey and the Bandit*, I put the pedal to the metal. Unfortunately, I came up behind the equivalent of *Sanford and Son*. Lamont had spent the whole day collecting treasures, and Fred was cautiously driving a good twenty miles under the speed limit. As an extra precaution for avoiding an accident and ensuring the safety of all the valuables, the junkmobile was straddling the divider lines in order to prevent anyone from passing. *Why me, Lord?*

Finally, after ten miles of excruciating pain, I made it to McDonalds, where I encountered Mrs. Grump. Apparently, her day had been worse than mine. While walking past the registers on the way to the porcelain oasis, her dirty-look dagger hit me squarely between the eyes. Ignoring it, I went about my business.

A few minutes later when I headed past the registers again, her suspicions were confirmed. I had only stopped in to use the restroom. Shame, shame, shame on me! Mrs. Grump was not pleased. In fact, she was quite angry and unwilling to let the moment pass without voicing her grievances.

"Excuse me, Ma'am?" She growled.

"Yes?" I turned.

She then bit my head off. "My restrooms are only for paying customers."

This was not a good day for pushing my buttons. Blood went to my face and sarcasm bit back through my fake-sweet voice. "First off, judging from your ever-so-typical bad-employee attitude, I seriously doubt that this is *your* restaurant or *your* restrooms, so let's get a grip as to your status on the Who's Who List in the McDonald's Hall of Fame, shall we? Second, in light of the hundreds of Happy Meals I've purchased over the years, I really don't think Ronald would mind my using his toilet without placing an order this one time." She was speechless. I left.

Now, I ask, how did my response to Mrs. Grump line up with God's command to consider others better than myself, to return evil with good, and to encourage those I encounter? Did my behavior earn a "good and faithful servant" pat on the back or an SUI citation? After I cooled off, a verse in Proverbs came to mind. "The words of the reckless pierce like swords, but the tongue of the wise brings healing" (12:18). Oh, the venom I can spew from my reckless tongue!

Had I taken time to *consider* my words in light of God's commands, I would have handled the situation much differently. I would have looked at this woman through the eyes of Jesus. Why was she so angry? What hard things in life had she suffered? Did her parents love her? Had someone hurt her? Had she been lied to all her life? Did she know the way to the Father who loves her more than anyone had ever loved her? Had she ever experienced the grace and mercies of God? Did she even know how she could?

Had I reined in my tongue and taken a few seconds to consider this precious creation of God rather than myself, I might have impacted her life for the sake of the gospel. I might have been used by God to change her life forever. I might have smiled warmly, purchased a drink, and asked her about her day. I might have spoken encouragement into her life and perhaps planted a seed of hope in her heart. But I didn't. God forgive me.

Now that I have confessed yet another time I behaved like a Christian jerk, please allow me to share about a time when I actually got it right. It happens from time to time, but be assured, it's only through God's grace in my life. I was pregnant with our second child. Because our first child arrived four weeks early, I was closely monitored during the last two trimesters. The nurse assigned to me either didn't like people in general or just didn't like me. She constantly made negative, insensitive comments. She was a Nazi when it came to taking prenatal vitamins, attending Lamaze class, and living by the book as a good pregnant woman. I broke all the rules. I was extremely sick all the way through my pregnancies. It was difficult for me to gain weight because I could rarely keep food down. While many women struggle with extra weight, I only gained baby weight, eleven pounds total with my second child. At eight months I looked like a green bean that had swallowed a basketball.

Nurse Nazi went down her chart checking "No" in answer to questions such as, "Have you faithfully taken your vitamins? Have you completed Lamaze? Will you be having the baby naturally without an epidural? Will you be breast-feeding?" With every answer her pen pressed a little harder on the chart, her eyebrows went a little higher, and her lips pressed a little tighter. I had not followed her rules. Then came the mean comments. "Well, on a positive note, I see that you've managed to stay nice and trim. Although that's not what's best for the baby, that cute little figure of yours will snap right back," she said in a voice dripping with sarcasm.

More subtle accusations were fired, but I had made up my mind to love Nurse Nazi regardless of how she treated me. Although I was tempted to retaliate, I chose not to criticize her bedside manners or personal hang-ups with rigid rule-following and thin women. I wanted God's love to flow through me to bless this woman. I overlooked her comments, took an interest in her life, asked questions that showed I cared, and spoke encouraging words into her heart. As I did those things, God gave me a love for this woman that passed understanding.

In the end Nurse Nazi and I shared a sweet bond. As overworked as she was, she requested to be my nurse during delivery and doted on me with extra acts of kindness, such as wiping my face with a cool cloth, fetching ice chips for me, and massaging my shoulders and legs. She became my labor room angel. What changed her attitude toward me? It wasn't me. It was the sweet, unconditional love of Christ working through me. It was a win-win situation for me and for her. Jesus did all the work, I got the benefit of shoulder and leg rubs, and Nurse Not-So-Nazi-Like-Anymore experienced the grace and mercies of the God who loves her. Not a bad deal.

God gives us the key for locking up critical words when we have been sinned against. It's called forbearance, and it's accomplished through love. Forbearance is an act of love and mercy that so completely covers wrongs committed against us that we truly forgive and forget. It chooses not to ponder the sins of others, especially the ones that inflict personal hurt, and instead dwells on how we might glorify God by blessing those around us regardless of their behavior.

At times forbearance is hardest to grant when the other person is your spouse. When your spouse sins against you with the fiery darts of unkind words, forbearance hurries to throw on a wet blanket. Forbearance does two things here: it covers the fire, protecting your mate from dangerous sparks, and it puts out the fire before it sets you ablaze, eliminating the possibility of an explosion.

In order to get a clear picture of forbearance, let's first take a look at what it is not. It is not shelving the sin to use as ammunition later. It is not begrudgingly ignoring the sin in order to take the high road. It is not pretending it did not happen in order to be the bigger person. It is not sulking secretly on the inside while outwardly faking kindness. These responses only reveal a type of self-serving, prideful retaliation that is not rooted in genuine love for the other person. They are rooted in the ground of self-preservation. In other words, they make us feel better about ourselves but accomplish nothing by way of the mercy, grace, and forgiveness that we are to offer through Christ.

Now let's look at what forbearance *is*. It is the willingness to overlook the offense and completely cast it away. It is the merciful choice to wipe the slate clean for the good of the other person. It is a love offering, folded in an envelope of true forgiveness and placed at the foot of the cross. It is the conscious outpouring of undeserved grace. It is the beautiful expression of mercy from a heart attitude of love.

I must caution you briefly on one point. Forbearance is not an excuse to avoid discussing or rebuking dangerous sin patterns in someone you love. Clearly, we are to lovingly rebuke those who are caught up in sin, to free them from enslavement. I know wives who sweep their husband's sin patterns under the rug due to a misguided understanding of forbearance. The forbearance I'm writing about is for minor offenses, such as a sharp word, something said in the heat of the moment, or a grouchy attitude. When we cover these types of personal offenses with forbearance, we demonstrate patience, wisdom, and love. Solomon said, "A person's wisdom yields patience; it is to one's glory to overlook an offense" (Prov. 19:11).

Perhaps the easiest time to succumb to the temptation of criticism is after we have been sinned against, yet we are warned not to "repay evil with evil or insult with insult. On the contrary, repay evil with blessing" (1 Peter 3:9). How do we do this? We take captive critical thoughts, making them obedient to Christ as soon as they enter our heads. Then we focus our attention on that which is excellent and praiseworthy—namely, the wonderful work God is doing in that person's life. To do this, we have to think before we speak. Because this is such a struggle for me, I often pray that the Holy Spirit would be the filter between my brain and my tongue.

When we have been sinned against, we have the option to retaliate with criticism, or cover it (or overwrite it) with love. Peter encourages us to do this: "Above all, love each other deeply, because love covers over a multitude of sins" (1 Peter 4:8). Not only does love cover a multitude of sins, but forbearance through love has preventive benefits for all. Solomon said, "Starting a quarrel is like breaching a dam; so drop the matter before a dispute breaks out" (Prov. 17:14). Forbearance nips a potential argument in the bud before it gets blown out of proportion. Historically, it is often the small battles that lead to war. The demonstration of forbearance rains peace on a potential battlefield before the armies ever rally to fight.

Another time when critical words spew from our lips is when things don't go our way, as with my Stinky State story at the beginning of this chapter. It's hard to voice encouraging words during not-so-ideal circumstances. How unimportant those circumstances would seem if our minds were truly set on eternity! They would melt away in light of the truth spoken to us in Romans through the apostle Paul: "I consider that our present sufferings are not worth comparing with the glory that will be revealed in us" (8:18).

How I long to be more like Paul when faced with trying situations! Acts 16 details how Paul and Silas preached the gospel in Philippi until they were dragged away, beaten, and bound in stocks in the inner cell of the jail. Yet, every time Paul remembered the Philippians, he was thankful. Paul had been in the worst of situations in Philippi. He suffered beatings and insults (1 Thess. 2:2), yet he continued to speak words of encouragement. How was Paul thankful and encouraging after such devastating, hard times? He *chose* to be.

Paul *chose* not to ponder aspects of the situation that would lead to the temptation of being critical. Instead, he set his mind and heart on things above. He determined to live out of the mercies and grace of God toward his adversaries in spite of his horrific circumstances. He resolved to dwell on the love he had for Jesus and the love Jesus had for him. Therefore, he was able to live out of the hope of the gospel.

Critical words begin with critical thinking. Critical thinking begins with a heart that lacks thankfulness for the goodness of God. God is good all the time, no matter what evils are happening around us or what circumstances we are facing. When we dwell on God's goodness during tough situations, it changes the way we view those situations and the way we handle them. Solomon encourages us not to search for the bad, but to seek out the good. He also indicates that there are consequences for both. "Whoever seeks good finds favor, but evil comes to one who searches for it" (Prov. 11:27). As sanctified children of God, we are empowered by the Holy Spirit to take captive critical thoughts and words, to edify others through speaking encouragement, and to live thankfully in the goodness of God.

The Proud Serial Sinner

and the Humble Grace of God

Normally, I do my grocery shopping in the morning while the store is not so crowded. But for whatever reason, I found myself waiting in the checkout line at 6:00 p.m. on Friday with my two children. The place was packed. There were cashiers at all ten registers and six or seven carts in every line. In the line next to me waited a mother and her two small children. They were about the same ages my children were at the time, three and five. Nearby was one of several mini-refrigerators, which were filled with various drinks and strategically located at the end of each checkout counter.

The five-year-old began to beg his mom for a Coke. (Let the games begin!)

Mom gave a firm "No." The boy began to walk over to the refrigerator.

Mom said loudly, "You had better not open that door!" The boy opened the door.

"You better not pull a drink out of there, mister!" The boy grabbed a Coke.

"If you open that Coke you are going to get it!" The boy unscrewed the cap, tossed it on the floor, and took a big swig.

Mom was screaming now, having completely lost it. "You just wait until we get home and your daddy hears about this! You kids never listen to me. I've had it up to here with you both!"

No one was able to decipher the exact location of "here," but we kept listening anyway. It's not that we were being nosy. It's just that there was nothing else to do while waiting in line, so this scene had the full attention of every customer. In order for bystanders to watch the scene unfold, they had to look past me and my children, who on this particular day were behaving well. Enter pride. Rather than having compassion for this poor mom and her struggles with her children, I smugly thought, *You won't see* my *kids acting like that.*

And then it happened. My three-year-old daughter Alex was standing right behind me when all of a sudden she blurted out the most horrible three words imaginable. It was as if she had grabbed one of the microphones from a checkout counter and yelled into it with all her might. Waving her hands frantically in front of her face, in a booming voice she screamed, "Mama! You pooted!" My entire body froze. Time stood still. To this day I don't know which was worse—the second she blurted it out or the minute it took for everyone to realize it was true.[2]

I am a living testimony of Proverbs 11:2, "When pride comes, then comes disgrace." Talk about your disgraceful moments.

My pride also brought me down a couple of years ago. A book came out by a well-known, popular author. I typically like his teaching and writing, but I didn't agree with some of the things he said in this particular book and I had been on a soapbox about it for weeks.

I was giving the keynote address at a homeschool convention in California. After the event, the convention hosts treated me to dinner at an upscale, elegant restaurant. I felt so important! The meal was fantastic and the conversation intriguing. The couple was extremely well-educated, well-spoken, and up-to-date on current events, so I was secretly thankful that they had not picked topics that were over my head to discuss. I wanted to give the impression of being on their level intellectually and, frankly, I was doing a pretty good job.

Then the husband asked if I had read so-and-so's newly released book. *Perfect!* I thought to myself and grinned. *I know I can impress them with my thoughts on this!* So I jumped in with both feet. "I didn't like it one bit," I announced, as I put down my fork and climbed on my familiar soapbox. I proceeded to rant over every little thing I disagreed with, paying no heed to uncomfortable squirms across the table. I went on, "I think fire kindling is the best use for that book." Then I went on some more. "As a matter of fact, I have lost all respect for this man as a writer, and if his next book were the last book on earth I wouldn't read it."

After thoroughly venting my opinion, satisfied that I had made *all* of my points, I smugly took a sip of coffee and asked, "Have you read the book yet?" Shifting in his seat and donning an expression that read, "I thought you'd never ask," he replied, "Well, actually, I was the editor of that book and the author is a very close friend of mine." I choked on my coffee. After several minutes of nursing a severe coughing frenzy, I finally regained enough composure to ask, "So, I guess I won't be keynoting again next year?"

Proud Serial Sinner: One who protects his own self-esteem, value, and dignity by denying his own sin, manufacturing tainted comparisons, and indulging in an overly high opinion of himself or herself.

The Humble Grace of God

Although a study of Christ's humility is beyond the scope of this chapter, I want to consider some brief examples. Jesus' greatest demonstration of humility was in his willingness to leave his heavenly kingdom, become man, and die for undeserving sinners like me. Paul records, "[Jesus] made himself nothing, by taking the very nature of a servant, being made in human likeness. And being found in appearance as a man, he humbled himself by becoming obedient to death—even death on a cross!" (Phil. 2:7-8).

His time on earth was not spent making demands or seeking honor. John records that Jesus said, "I do not accept glory from human beings" (5:41), and he made it clear that his purpose for humbling himself was not to do his own will, but the will of the Father (6:38). He did not come to receive honor and praise, but avoided it like the plague. "After the people saw the sign Jesus performed, they began to say, 'Surely this is the Prophet who is to come into the world.' Jesus, knowing that they intended to come and make him king by force, withdrew again to a mountain by himself" (John 6:14-15).

I don't know about you, but if I knew someone was coming to bestow an honor on me or make me queen for the day, the only place I'd go is to get my hair done so that it would fashionably accommodate the crown. But not Jesus. He was not here for that purpose. When he made his entry into Jerusalem, he didn't ride in on a tall, white stallion demanding trumpets and confetti. Matthew records, "See, your king comes to you, gentle and riding on a donkey, on a colt, the foal of a donkey" (Matt. 21:5).

When his accusers stripped him, beat him, spit in his face, pulled out his beard, forced a crown of thorns into his head, and led him to be crucified, he did not retaliate. He could have stopped them with one word, but he didn't. Isaiah tells us, "He was oppressed and afflicted, yet he did not open his mouth; he was led like a lamb to the slaughter, and as a sheep before its shearers is silent, so he did not open his mouth" (53:7).

The Gospels tell how Jesus demonstrated humility from start to finish. He was born in a manger, lived in poverty, submitted to ordinances, and befriended the despised. He willingly suffered (Isa. 50:6) and died a humiliating death on our behalf (Heb. 12:2). To imagine that the King of kings and Lord of lords left his heavenly throne for such humiliation as this astounds me. I am grateful for the undeserved grace given to me through his sacrificial display of humility.

God Calls Christians to Humility

Throughout Scripture, God calls Christians to be humble, saying that he "opposes the proud, but shows favor to the humble" (James 4:6). He warns of the consequences of pride, "For those who exalt themselves will be humbled" and foretells of the blessings of humility, "Those who humble themselves will be exalted" (Matt. 23:12). He explains that humility is a prerequisite for his guidance in our lives (Ps. 25:9) and that we are to wrap it around everything we do (Col. 3:12).

Humility is hard. Without Christ living through us, it is impossible. We will talk more about that later, but the first step toward understanding biblical humility is to acknowledge how pride reigns in the hearts of Christians. It's there, but it's the hardest sin to admit because it is the ugliest. It is the granddaddy of all sins—typically the sin from which all other sins originate. It was pride that caused Satan to become Satan. It was pride that caused the fall of Israel. And—as much as we hate to admit it—it is often pride that blocks the Holy Spirit from moving in our lives.

Pride was the motive behind the first sin ever committed (Gen. 3:4-5), and it comes first on God's list of the seven things he absolutely hates (Prov. 6:16-17). Here's the clincher: the more you deny your struggle with it, the greater it is in your heart. Your eagerness to simply dismiss it reveals the strength of its hold on your heart. It's the sin with the strongest grip, the sin we loathe most when we see it in others, and the sin we refuse to see in ourselves. Let's look at these last two points.

Pride is the sin we loathe most when we see it in others. I once dated a fellow who drove me up the wall with his boasting. He would ask, "What did you think of that touchdown I made? Have you ever seen anybody run so fast and dodge so many people before crossing into the end zone?" He invited me to go to the beach one weekend with his family by saying, "If it's okay with you, my dad will fly us down in our fifteen-passenger Lear jet, and we can spend a couple of days on our seven-and-a-half-million-dollar yacht, which by the way, is the largest one in the Florida Keys." After three months of dating, I was ready to slap some duct tape on his mouth, bind his hands and feet, and throw him off his seven-and-a-half-million-dollar yacht.

The more pride we have, the more we despise it in others. While this boy desperately needed to get over himself, I must admit that I am guilty of this same sort of boasting. I'm just slightly more clever in how I do it. I've manipulated conversations in order to casually mention an accomplishment, name drop, or detail a "humble" act of service. I've said things like, "I am so excited! I've been invited to speak at the largest homeschool convention in the country." Realizing how that might sound, I'll quickly add a spiritual cover-up to divert attention from my proud motive. "What an amazing opportunity to encourage others for God's glory." I may have fooled the listener, but I certainly haven't fooled God. The sin is there, but thankfully, his response is to point me to repentance, forgiveness, and atonement. *Lord, where would I be without your amazing grace? Please convict and cleanse my heart of pride.*

When King Nebuchadnezzar warned, "And those who walk in pride [God] is able to humble" (Dan. 4:37), he wasn't kidding. I was attending the Christian Booksellers Association Convention (now named the International Christian Retail Show) a few years ago, where many famous writers are in residence for the week. After chatting with Frank Peretti, Francine Rivers, John Tesh, Dennis Rainey, and Rick Warren (see, there I go again), my head had grown three sizes too big for my shoulders. There I was, rubbing shoulders with some of the most well-known, influential people in our country. Francine had even shared details with me about the book she was working on. Boy, was I puffed up! Feeling like I was really in the know, I arrogantly strutted toward a group of writers who were talking and aggressively joined their conversation.

After a few minutes, I turned to the man beside me, confidently stuck out my hand, and said, "Hi, I don't believe I know you. What's your name and what do you do?" All conversations came to a screeching halt. Everyone looked at me as if I were a green three-headed alien. The man on the other end of my outstretched hand was Tim LaHaye, author of the best-selling *Left Behind* series. I doubt there was a single person at that convention who hadn't recognized him. While everyone else was trying to figure out how I had gotten past security, this precious man of God humbly answered, "What did I do, you ask? I married Beverly LaHaye." What a sweet answer to my utterly stupid question.

Pride is the sin we refuse to see in ourselves. As I mentioned earlier, it is often so well disguised that it's hard to recognize it as the fuel behind many sins. A man standing in line at the store, gazing at the photo of a woman on a magazine cover may recognize his lust, but pride is behind it. In his imagination the woman desires him as much as he desires her. After all, it takes two to tango! In using her image for his own pleasure, fantasizing that she lusts after him, he assumes, "This woman wants me!" Pride.

Meanwhile, a woman looking at the same magazine cover may envy the body of the woman in the photograph, harbor jealousy over the attention that body attracts, and experience discontentment with her own body. She may recognize her envy, jealousy, or discontent with her own body, but not the pride behind it. She wants to be admired just like the woman on the cover. When we do certain activities—including exercising or losing weight—with the underlying motive of gaining the admiration of others, pride is the source.

Many of us have issues with certain features of our bodies. Some fuss over hips. Some fuss over hair. Some fuss over legs. My most self-despised and hideously ugly feature was my pea-sized baby tooth. Yes, I had a thirty-seven-year-old baby tooth. It was in front and getting browner every year. Notice how I speak of it in past tense. This is because my vanity finally got the better of me.

I decided to take the plunge—have it pulled and replaced with a bridge. Have you ever heard that if you redecorate one room in your house it makes the other rooms look bad? Well, it's the same with teeth. The new one looked so good that it aroused a discontentment in me toward all the others. I decided to satisfy my vain longing for perfect teeth by purchasing porcelain veneers. After all, money can't buy love, but it certainly can buy some pretty nice teeth.

What I didn't realize was that preparation for veneers involves the utter destruction of all teeth involved. Just before the procedure, my dentist explained that he would file down my natural teeth to thin, pointy little things (my paraphrase). Then he would glue in temporary teeth while the veneers were being made, which would take a couple of weeks. I would have backed out at this point, but he quickly assured me that no one would ever see them as "pointy little things" because he would install the fabulous-looking temporaries immediately after filing.

The temporaries had only been in a couple of days. I was extremely pleased with how good they looked, often admiring myself with a movie star smile while purposefully passing by mirrors in the house. I beamed with pride even more when I thought of how the permanent ones would make my smile even more glamorous. Because I spent much of the day admiring my new appearance and anticipating all of the compliments I was sure to receive, I neglected to cook supper. *That's okay*, I thought. *It's Friday night. I'll kick off the weekend by having a supreme pizza delivered for dinner.* Of course, I made sure to smile extra big for the delivery boy. Much to my chagrin, he seemed far more interested in my five-dollar tip than my five-thousand-dollar smile. Ridiculous, I know.

I stole one more admiring look in the dining room mirror before serving the piping hot pizza. *Oh yeah*, I rhythmically nodded to the cool '80s rock-and-roll beat playing in my head. I piled the pizza on my plate. Suddenly, like the walls of Jericho, all my pride came tumbling down. The Lord giveth and the Lord taketh away. I bit into a slice of pizza and my teeth literally fell out of my mouth. I looked down and found them lying on my chest covered in marinara and melted cheese. Horrified, I covered my mouth, ran to the mirror in my bathroom and burst into tears as I yelled, "Oh . . . no! I look like Sméagol from *Lord of the Rings*!"

My dentist wouldn't be in until Monday, so I decided to make the best of it. I roamed through the house all weekend grinning at my kids and whispering, "Myyy precious," which caused them to run from me and scream, "Stop, Mom! You're freaking us out!" So much for glamor.

The next two weeks were a nightmare. My teeth continually fell out and had to be glued back in every three to four days. One night I woke up around 3:00 a.m. only to find that they had fallen out and my Yorkie was chewing on them. Oh, the things we do for vanity!

Vanity is a form of pride that is fairly easy to detect. However, there are many ways pride shows itself without our detecting it. How about when we monopolize the conversation? We may argue, "I'm just not a good listener" or "I have trouble focusing when others are talking" or "I'm just keeping the conversation going." But pride is the root. This sort of pride says, "I believe that what I have to say is more important and more worthy of being heard. I am always right, I have all the answers, and I do not have time to listen to your insignificant thoughts."

Another display of pride appears when we finish sentences for others, cut them off before they are done, or become frustrated or impatient while waiting for them to finish a thought. This pride says, "I am smarter and pick up things faster. Therefore, I shouldn't have to wait for you to sort through this in your slow-thinking mind."

How about when we avoid people who don't appeal to us? Many of us tend to hang with those who are most like us. We pause long enough to "help" those in need, but don't really consider them our friends. I am so convicted of this. I want God to change me and I am thankful that he is working on me. My natural tendency is to pal around with people who appeal to me, people I have fun with. Sure, I take time out to "minister," but to really invest in a friendship with some people would go against my nature. I prefer to be around those who think like me, act like me, appreciate my humor, and mesh with my personality. If someone doesn't fit that bill, then deep within my wicked heart, I think they are not worthy of my time and attention. *Oh, Jesus! Apart from you I am nothing but a wicked, vile sinner. I am convicted and ashamed. Please don't turn away from my sinful pride, but help me to be more like you.*

Be honest. Look deeply into your heart and consider if you have ever thought yourself better than someone else. How about the person with a life-controlling addiction? How about the uneducated? How about those who are poverty-stricken or homeless? Can you sincerely say, "Those people are equal to me," or do you secretly think, *I am not, nor will I ever be, like them because I am better than that*? Jesus said that to think such a thing is pride, but I dare say many of us consider ourselves better than certain people. Perhaps not as good as some, but definitely better than others. Even as a nation, we struggle with a better-than-you attitude toward other countries. We are blessed with a higher standard of living, which forms the basis for our judging other nationalities. The apostle Paul, knowing our sinful tendencies toward this sort of thinking, said, "in humility value others above yourselves" (Phil. 2:3).

Jesus warned us about viewing ourselves more highly than others in a parable. He said, "Two men went up to the temple to pray, one a Pharisee and the other a tax collector. The Pharisee stood by himself and prayed: 'God, I thank you that I am not like other people—robbers, evildoers, adulterers—or even like this tax collector. I fast twice a week and give a tenth of all I get.' But the tax collector stood at a distance. He would not even look up to heaven, but beat his breast and said, 'God, have mercy on me, a sinner.' I tell you that this man, rather than the other, went home justified before God. For all those who exalt themselves will be humbled, and those who humble themselves will be exalted" (Luke 18:10-14).

"I would never say such a thing!" you might say in your own defense. I wouldn't either—but I have thought it. Sometimes we think we're safe in our thoughts. We think it doesn't count if we don't say it, but there is no hiding from God. He knew us before we were born, he knows every hair on our heads, and he knows every sinful thought and attitude in our hearts. We are told in Scripture, "People look at the outward appearance, but the LORD looks at the heart" (1 Sam. 16:7). *God, have mercy on my soul.*

The good news is that we don't have to struggle with pride. Those who truly know Jesus are no longer its slaves. We have been washed clean through the blood of Christ, and our shame is no more. We are *guiltless.* Our sins are gone. They have been cast away from us. The Bible tells us, "As far as the east is from the west, so far has he removed our transgressions from us" (Ps. 103:12). We can walk freely and blamelessly without the sin of pride because Jesus has won victory over sin on our behalf.

Does this mean that our struggle with pride is over? No. Pride is our weakness. Yet it is through our weaknesses that God manifests his strength and ongoing work in our lives. When we acknowledge and confess weakness rather than denying it, the Holy Spirit brings about repentance, which brings about God's righteousness in us. Jesus said, "My grace is sufficient for you, for my power is made perfect in weakness." As a result of this wonderful promise from Jesus, Paul said, "Therefore I will boast all the more gladly about my weaknesses, so that Christ's power may rest on me. That is why, for Christ's sake, I delight in weaknesses, in insults, in hardships, in persecutions, in difficulties. For when I am weak, then I am strong" (2 Cor. 12:9-10).

Embracing this wonderful truth brings freedom. It's the freedom to forget about ourselves and lay down our measuring rods of self-worth and ongoing scrutiny. It's the freedom to release the suffocating anxiety our weaknesses cause, and instead take hold of God's grace given to us through the cross. It's the freedom to genuinely live out of the gospel of Jesus Christ with an authentic, humble love that is evident to all people in all walks of life. Whether rich or poor, educated or ignorant, a perfect "ten" or a social outcast, we can know that when we reach out to others with this kind of authentic, humble love, we are doing the will of the Father and the work of the kingdom.

The Controlling Serial Sinner

and the Sovereign Grace of God

Hi, my name is Ginger Hubbard, and I'm an obsessive-compulsive control freak. There, I said it. They say the first step to recovery is admission. I'll take it a step further and tell you that I have always been controlling. I was born with a director's baton, and I've been leading the band ever since. I was a bossy child, always insisting that everyone play when I wanted to play, what I wanted to play, and how I wanted to play. Boys two feet taller than me would tremble and jump at my command. My poor neighborhood friends! Even when pretending, they were forced at tongue-point to play within the grand ideas of my imagination, never theirs.

My younger brother also was a victim of my control. I actually rewrote the rules to Monopoly, granting him the privilege of playing the new and improved version—Gin-opoly. Wisely, he never bucked the rules, even when they periodically changed in my favor.

As a dating teen, I announced where we would eat and which movie we would see. It was also understood that I would do the driving since I preferred my own car to anyone else's. I would pick up my date and I would drop him off. If I decided he could kiss me goodnight, I would walk him to the door. If not, he was merely instructed to make sure the car door shut completely as he got out. My boyfriends' mothers didn't like me. Go figure.

As a mother, I've caused frustrations for my children through my desire to be in control, especially with schoolwork. While teachers in public and private school systems generally require about 80 percent of a textbook to be completed, my controlling personality leans toward an attack-and-conquer mentality. When my children wanted to know why they couldn't take off a full week for Thanksgiving or two weeks for Christmas like all the other homeschooled children, I answered, "How can you finish every page in every book if you take that much time off?" It made perfect sense to me, but for whatever reason it didn't fly well with them.

I've also been guilty of trying to control their feelings and opinions. It was easy when they were young and believed that Mommy was brilliant. However, as they got older, their ever-developing discernment warned them that this might not be true. Dang that discernment! Crept right in and ruined my reign.

God has taught me a few lessons about trying to control the opinions of my children, particularly through my daughter Alex, who is most like me (Lord, help her). Like Elly May Clampett of the *Beverly Hillbillies* television show, Alex has an unusual way with animals. Recently she believed that the wild geese swimming reluctantly up to the pier at our lake house would eat from her hand. "Honey," I said with a know-it-all chuckle, "you can throw bread crumbs out to them, but they're not going to swim close enough to eat out of your. . . ." My words trailed off as two geese swam right up and ate from her hand. God is in control, not me.

The same sort of thing happened with Gary the Goldfish. Growing tired of cleaning his bowl, Alex decided to set Gary free in the creek behind our house. Having a soft spot for even the smallest of creatures, I rebuked Alex for not thinking through the consequences that poor Gary would suffer. "No, Mom, I have it all figured out. I know Gary doesn't know how to find his own food, so I plan on meeting him by the bridge and feeding him every day," she insisted. Determined to change her naive, ten-year-old opinion, I reminded her of the mileage of the creek, the strength of the current, and the size of Gary's brain. Not to mention the much larger, wild fish lurking around in search of glistening goldfish snacks. "Well, I think he'll meet me at the bridge and will make friends with all the other fish," Alex stated with certainty.

Would you believe that crazy fish hung out near the bridge for two weeks, eating every meal Alex provided him? Well, believe it. I went to the creek with her and saw it with my own eyes. The minute we walked onto the bridge, Gary swam up eagerly. Even more shocking, he brought with him a whole passel of friends, all shapes and sizes. They shared the meal together, and then swam off, their little tail fins wagging as if to say, "Thanks, Alex! See you next time!" It beat all I've ever seen. God is in control, not me.

I won't even go into the whole story of how she kept a baby deer in the house for a week. Rescued from being attacked by dogs in our backyard, the deer behaved more like a tamed puppy than a wild animal around Alex. His last night in our home involved the two of them sitting on the couch together, watching *Bambi* and eating popcorn. I have pictures.

My son Wesley has not escaped my manipulative, controlling tactics. "Don't you think this blue shirt looks better on you?" I would ask, in spite of the fact that he prefers the burnt-orange one. A more motive-revealing question might be, "Don't you think my taste is better than yours?"

As a teen, Wesley enjoys rearranging the furniture in his room from time to time. In my opinion there is one way it looks best. "Don't you think it looks more spacious the other way?" I ask. "I think it's spacious this way too," he replies with all due respect. "But don't you think it looks better the other way?" I come back. A more motive-revealing question might be, "Why don't you agree with my opinion and keep it the way I like it?"

Even more trying is giving up control in marriage. Kim (not her real name) explained her struggle to control not only her husband's actions, but also his thinking. Kim confessed how her husband wanted to branch out on a business venture with which she disagreed. "I was afraid he was making a bad decision so I tried to talk him out of it. And more than that, I not only wanted to talk him out of it, I wanted him to *agree* with me. I wanted to control his actions and his thinking as well. I realize now that my need to be in control of John's thinking stemmed from a selfish narrow-mindedness. His difference of opinion meant that I would have to consider the possibility of being wrong. Since I don't like being wrong, my self-righteousness and inflated ego demanded that he agree with me."

I, too, have struggled with control to the point of not respecting the differing opinions of others. Once my mind is made up regarding an issue, I want everyone around me to not only understand my point of view, but to adopt it. I once heard a comedian who pegged me (and many other women) when he described a woman's motive for discussing things with her husband: "Women don't want to hear what you think. Women want to hear what they think—in a deeper voice!"

I have a hard time being at rest with an opinion that differs from mine. I tend to roll it over and over in my mind, looking at every angle until I can justify being right. The controlling side of me wants to believe that my way is the only right way. I've always had a talent for persuading others to accept my way of thinking. I am a master convincer. Someone once told me I could sell a Bible to the Devil.

Kim continued her story. "God has shown me that my need to be in control is nothing more than a lack of trust in his sovereignty. I was fearful of John making a wrong decision. I envisioned his business deal going south, us selling our home and automobiles and moving into a cardboard box in a dark alley. But when I fear the consequences of John's decisions, I am putting my confidence in John rather than God. When I try to control John's decisions, I am putting my confidence in myself rather than God. Only in trusting that God is ultimately in control can I truly rest. Should things turn out badly, I can still trust that God is good, in control, and that he will care for me. God promises, 'The Lord is good, a refuge in times of trouble. He cares for those who trust in him' (Nah. 1:7). He is trustworthy all the time, good times and bad.

"I am also learning to pour out my heart to God, rather than being so quick to try and control John. The psalmist encouraged, 'Trust him at all times, O people; pour out your hearts to him, for God is our refuge' (Ps. 62:8). When I pray and trust, I can rest in his sovereignty no matter the outcome."

We can't be certain that when we pour out our hearts to God, trust him, and surrender control, circumstances will always turn out to our liking. However, we *can* be certain they will turn out in accordance with God's will. We can be confident that even when things don't work out well, God still uses situations to bring us closer to him. We can know that he is working on something far greater than we can understand. Isaiah encouraged, "The Lord is the everlasting God, the Creator of the ends of the earth. He will not grow tired or weary, and his understanding no one can fathom" (40:28).

Kim concluded, "For years, while I thought I was holding on to control, control was holding me. It kept me imprisoned in anxiety. I would worry and fret over John's decisions and my insides churned in turmoil as I lived in a constant state of stress. It was only through surrendering control and trusting God, regardless of how things might turn out, that I began to experience peace and rest. I believe it is a peace and rest that can reign even in the heart of one living in a cardboard box."

Controlling Serial Sinner: An obsessive, manipulative power seeker with an inflated ego, who exercises self-appointed authority or dominating influence to ensure personal interests and desired outcomes.

The Sovereign Grace of God

God is sovereign over all creation. He foresaw the beginning, he foresees the end, and he is fully aware of everything that happens in between. Paul testified, "For in him all things were created: things in heaven and on earth, visible and invisible, whether thrones or powers or rulers or authorities; all things have been created through him and for him" (Col. 1:16). It is through his sovereignty that he foreknew us before we were born (Rom. 8:29-30). He is sovereign over the church (Col. 1:18), over life (Gen. 1:27), over death (Matt. 9:23-25), over weather (Matt. 8:23-26), over evil (Matt. 8:28-29), and over time (2 Peter 3:8). Entire books have been dedicated to the study of God's knowledge and revelation of events before they happen. Every fulfilled prophecy in Scripture testifies to the sovereignty of God. He is all knowing and all powerful.

Through many circumstances, God has taught me about his sovereignty. He has shown me how important it is to let go of the steering wheel of life and trust him.

God has certainly taught me to trust him through his outpouring of blessing, but he has also taught me to trust him through his outpouring of sustaining grace in times of trouble. One unforgettable instance readily comes to mind.

When I answered my cell phone, the voice on the other end didn't sound human. I could not decipher who it was. "Calm down and speak slowly," I repeated to no avail. Finally, I recognized the desperate sobs of my sister-in-law Gina. My face twisted in pain as I knew something terrible was about to rock my world. "Benji's not breathing!" Gina wailed, "His body is blue and he's not breathing!" *Oh Jesus, please, Jesus!* my heart cried. "I'll meet you at the hospital," I choked through a tightened throat. As my vision blurred and my legs turned to clay, running to my car was like running underwater. Everything was happening in slow motion, and it seemed an eternity before I came to a screeching halt just outside the emergency room. I bolted past the front desk and charged through the double doors, knowing in my heart that my ten-week-old nephew had left this world forever.

Our families huddled together, pleading with Jesus to "let this cup pass" as doctors and nurses worked for over an hour trying to revive our beloved Benji. Then came the most dreadful, gut-wrenching words a parent could ever hear: "I'm sorry, we did everything we could. He's gone." Gina crumbled to the floor. Inhuman noises echoed from her throat as grief like I have never heard forced its way out. Pain so deep that it sucked the air from my lungs and shook my body as I held Gina in my arms.

What took place after Benji's death had God's sovereignty written all over it. Gina, my brother Steven, as well as my whole family, experienced God's grace at a level unknown to many. We were embraced by the comforting arms of Jesus, sustained by the soothing Word of God, and filled with peace that passes understanding.

God's grace was poured out during the funeral, which was held on the day of Steven and Gina's sixth anniversary. As the same soloist who sang "There Is a Redeemer" on their wedding day sang it at their baby boy's funeral, a comforting assurance washed over me. I knew God was just as faithful as he had always been. The Redeemer who celebrated in their joy is the same Redeemer who would hold them in sorrow. The music played on, and when my precious sister-in-law tilted her head upward and lifted her hands to worship Jesus, God's presence came down like I had never witnessed before.

The doctors said Benji died of SIDS. I say Benji's heavenly Father looked upon his sleeping body that Thursday morning and proclaimed through tears of joy, "This one's mine." Not only did Benji trade the pain and suffering of this world for the magnificent glories of heaven, but he also was used more powerfully for God's glory after a mere ten weeks of life than most of us will be used in a lifetime. Steven and Gina have glorified God in a way that would not have been possible had Benji remained on earth.

Steven, Gina, and my parents own a popular restaurant in our community. Through it, our family knows many people in our community and they know us. We were blessed when people from all walks of life attended the funeral. There were young and old, rich and poor, lost and saved. What they witnessed was a family with hope. They saw much more than a grieving young couple who would miss their baby boy in the painful days ahead. They saw a sovereign and faithful God who keeps his promises; a God who comforts those who mourn and gives hope to those who receive him as Savior and Lord. "I came to the funeral in such despair," one woman shared, "but I left with such hope." "I want to know God the way your family knows him," said another. "I never thought there was much to religion, but I saw something different from religion at Benji's funeral," admitted an acquaintance. "I want to understand more about who God is," explained a nurse. Letters, phone calls, and visitors have confirmed the beauty of God's sovereignty, the goodness of his will, and the perfection of his plan.

I am reminded of my four-year-old niece's words as she held my mother's hand and stared at the twenty-nine-inch coffin that held her baby brother. It was shiny and white with lovely spring flowers draped over the top. With innocent curiosity she asked, "Nana, is that a present for Jesus?" Certain of her answer, my mother replied, "Yes, Baby, it is . . . it most certainly is."

What did I learn through this painful experience? God is sovereign and in control of all things. There is nothing we can do to change the will of God. We can trust God when he gives, and we can trust God when he takes away. He is the almighty giver of joy in good times and the almighty giver of joy in bad times. He is Creator, Sustainer, and Redeemer. He is the beginning and the end. He is good.

God Calls Christians to Trust

Dr. Jere Colley is a well-respected veterinarian in my hometown of Opelika, Alabama. Everyone loves Dr. Colley. He is the kind of person who would do anything for anyone. He loves people, he loves animals, and he loves God. Dr. Colley has the biggest heart of anyone I know.

Because he is a problem solver, it's hard for Dr. Colley not to be an "in-control" person. After all, he solves problems to make a living. When a pet is hurting or needs some sort of treatment, Dr. Colley is your man. He assesses the condition, makes a decision, and administers the proper medication. He takes control of the situation and fixes the problem. While he is good at what he does, he once told me of a time when taking control backfired on him.

A young boy and his dad walked into the clinic one morning. The boy was so upset that he could barely control his voice. In his trembling hands was a small, gray hamster. Dr. Colley recalled, "Ginger, I took one look at that hamster and I knew he was on his last leg." With a quivering bottom lip, the little boy pleaded, "Please, Dr. Colley, please make my hamster better. He's really sick, but I know you can fix him and make him better again." Dr. Colley's heart melted as the child, with tears streaming down his face, placed his furry little companion into the doctor's hand. At that moment the hamster exhaled the air from his struggling lungs, laid his head over, and died.

Covering the deceased with his other hand so the boy couldn't see, Dr. Colley made a decision. "I tell you what, son," he said. "Have Dad take you to get some ice cream. Give me about an hour, and let me see what I can do." The boy's dad reluctantly guided his son to the door, glancing back at Dr. Colley as if he had lost his mind. As soon as they exited the parking lot, Dr. Colley jumped in his car, drove to the local pet store, and purchased a hamster the same size and color as the boy's hamster.

The boy never knew the difference. "Thank you! Thank you! Thank you, Dr. Colley!" the child enthusiastically shouted as he held his lively, energetic hamster. Satisfied that his plan had worked, Dr. Colley went about the rest of his day whistling happy tunes. He was surprised to receive a call from the boy's dad that night. "Jere!" he blurted, "I can't believe you! I've been waiting three years for that hamster to die, and there you go buying him a brand new one!"

We all think we can fix things and make things better. While I pick on kind-hearted Dr. Colley (with his permission), I'm convinced that women are the worst at trying to control situations. Take Sarai, for example. Sarai wanted nothing more than to have children with her husband Abram. Sarai pleaded with God to give her a child, but she still didn't become pregnant. Therefore, as we do at times, Sarai decided to take matters into her own hands.

Genesis records, "Now Sarai, Abram's wife, had borne him no children. But she had an Egyptian slave named Hagar; so she said to Abram, 'The LORD has kept me from having children. Go, sleep with my slave; perhaps I can build a family through her'" (16:1-2). In other words, "God has kept me from having children, but surely he has made some sort of a mistake. Since God doesn't know what he's doing, I had better take control of the situation." Sarai was so desperate that she ordered her husband to sleep with another woman. Blinded by her own desire to have a child, she made a terrible, foolish mistake.

It's easy for us to write off Sarai as a woman who had gone off the deep end. However, many of us are guilty of the same mindset. We might not consider arranging a romantic evening for our husband and another woman in order to have a child, but how many of us have controlled a situation with words or actions to manipulate the outcome? We convince ourselves that we know best. Then we take control. Like Sarai, we become so blinded by our own desires and so wrapped up in controlling an outcome that we make terrible mistakes.

How did the honorable Abram respond to Sarai's idea? The Scriptures record, "Abram agreed to what Sarai said" (16:2). Now that's a shocker! I'll bet if God would have confronted him after the dirty deed Abram would have said, "I had no choice! It was that woman you gave me that made me do it!" Uh-huh, whatever. The story goes on to say, "So after Abram had been living in Canaan ten years, Sarai his wife took her Egyptian slave Hagar and gave her to her husband to be his wife. He slept with Hagar, and she conceived. When she knew she was pregnant, she began to despise her mistress" (16:3-4).

The spool unraveled. The games began! Before we look at the rest of the story, let's assess the probable emotional state of the women involved. On one hand is a wife who is dealing with her emotions about manipulating her husband into sleeping with another woman; she is also probably jealous that Hagar could conceive. On the other hand is a hormonal, pregnant slave girl who feels used and has more than likely become emotionally attached to a man who belongs to another woman. It was a recipe for disaster. And that's exactly what it cooked up.

What did Sarai do when things began to fall apart? You'll find this interesting. The passage reads, "Then Sarai said to Abram, 'You are responsible for the wrong I am suffering'" (16:5). Her response is laughable. The whole scam was her idea, but when it didn't unfold to her liking, she blamed Abram. Of course, at the outset, I doubt Abram saw his role in the plan as the short end of the stick, "Sure, honey, I'll have sex with her if it'll make you happy. It'll be tough and I probably won't enjoy it, but I'd do anything for you, sweetheart."

Sarai continued her ranting, "I put my slave in your arms, and now that she knows she is pregnant, she despises me. May the LORD judge between you and me" (16:5). Sadly, Sarai concluded her rampage by calling down judgment on her marriage. The outcome was devastating. Hagar had a son and named him Ishmael. He was described as a "wild donkey of a man" (16:12). He was full of hate, stirring up dissension all the days of his life. Sarai and Abram suffered the consequences of not trusting God with their family.

The chaotic and sad outcome of this story teaches us that no matter how badly we want something or how great we think our plan is to fix a situation, it is always better to simply trust God and let him be in control of our lives. Why do we struggle with surrendering control and trusting God? I believe it is because we think too highly of ourselves. We see part of the picture and think we know what's best. We become confident in our own abilities and conceited to the point of thinking that our ways are better than God's way. That's exactly what happened to King Saul.

When Saul first became king, he trusted God rather than himself. He listened to God, depended on him, and did what God told him to do. However, after situations had been going well for a while, Saul began to get cocky. He started convincing himself, "Hey, I've got the hang of this king of Israel thing. I've gotten good at what I do. I keep things pretty well under control, and I'm sure I can handle it without God from here on out." However, as soon as Saul decided he didn't need God anymore and Israel's theme song became "I Did It My Way," things began to fall apart.

One particular instance where Saul chose to take control was after God commanded him to kill the Amalekites, including all their livestock (1 Sam. 15:3). Samuel confronted Saul after the battle and asked whether he had fully obeyed God. Saul uttered an affirmative reply, but unfortunately for Saul, Samuel could hear the bleating of sheep in the background. Saul had not trusted or obeyed God. God had been clear that Saul was to kill the livestock, but Saul kept some of the livestock for himself. I'm sure Saul rationalized his decision: "Why waste all that livestock? What good would that do?"

As we do sometimes, Saul tried to justify his actions. He tried to reason with Samuel by saying that he only kept some livestock to offer as sacrifices to God. This sounds noble, doesn't it? I would have bought it, but Samuel didn't. Samuel, being a man who trusted God no matter how illogical it seemed, rebuked Saul by saying, "To obey is better than sacrifice" (1 Sam. 15:22). Because Saul took matters into his own hands and left God out, he lost his position as king (15:26-28). Saul suffered severe consequences for not trusting God.

I look at Saul's foolish choices and see myself. Do you? Have you ever done something you knew was wrong, but rather than confessing, you tried to justify your actions to God or others? Justifying our actions when we know they're wrong is nothing more than an attempt to control the way we are viewed. To gain the approval of others, we try to manipulate their opinion of us through self-justification. If we're honest, I believe we would all have to admit we've done this to some degree.

Also like Saul, we become confident that we can assess situations and make good decisions without consulting God. We think we can fix things on our own and make things right. It's not that our motives are bad. They're usually quite good. However, God wants us to trust him and not manipulate situations to get the results we think are best. He wants us to rest our anxious hearts and relinquish control to him, the Creator of the universe. In his sovereignty, God sees the whole picture—the one we can't see. As a result, his perspective differs from ours.

Life becomes more of a grand adventure when we let go of control and trust God. This lesson came at a time when I least expected it, and it involved a tremendous leap of faith.

Nausea swelled in my gut as I watched my eight-year-old, thrill-seeking daughter, Alex, stand at the ticket booth. Why anyone would want to experience falling through the sky only to be yanked back up into the air by a bungee cord just before splattering all over the concrete is beyond me. Everyone enjoys a good thrill ride from time to time, but relying on a bungee cord to continue living is taking it a bit too far, in my opinion.

"Are you sure you want to do this, honey?" asked the concerned man in the ticket booth. "We do have go-carts and bumper boats that someone your age might find more enjoyable." With chin up, hands planted firmly on her hips and a stubborn look of determination that I recognized all too well, my petite, blonde fireball assured the man that she was brave enough to jump. "What if you get scared when you get to the top and change your mind?" the gentleman asked as he reluctantly handed her the ticket. "Don't worry, I won't," Alex shot back. And somehow, I knew she wouldn't.

"Have you ever lost anyone?" I asked. "Not yet, but we've only been open for three weeks," the man replied with a grin. Perfect.

Without hesitation, Alex ran from the ticket booth to the bungee harness, eager to take the plunge. As her little body plummeted through the night sky with screams of excitement, I thought, "Lord, what's it going to take to thrill her when she's sixteen?"

She didn't wait until she was sixteen. She waited until she was fourteen. She piled into a boat with her seventeen-year-old brother, a posse of friends and headed for Lake Martin's famous Chimney Rock, where adventure seekers from all over jump from its sixty-foot cliff into the water. I was horrified when they came back to the lake house and my son informed me in an unnerved voice, "Mom! Alex climbed to the top of Chimney Rock. She didn't even hesitate! She just leaped right off!" While I was not okay with her poor choice, once I recovered from the shock, it hit me that thrill-seeking can definitely be used for God's glory. "Father, may she find this much delight in taking leaps of faith that please you."

Like Alex, Peter had a longing for adventure. His longing was rooted in a desire to trust God. When the disciples' boat was being tossed about by threatening winds, they became alarmed. Their fear level peaked when they saw a man walking on water toward the boat. The man was Jesus. That's when Peter seized the opportunity for an ultimate thrill. Peter requested that Jesus call him to walk on water. Peter's desire to walk on water in spite of his fear was based not only on his passion for adventure, but his passion to trust God in an adventurous way.

When Jesus told Peter to come, he jumped from the boat without hesitating. Matthew records, "Then Peter got down out of the boat, walked on the water and came toward Jesus. But when he saw the wind, he was afraid and, beginning to sink, cried out, 'Lord, save me!' Immediately Jesus reached out his hand and caught him. 'You of little faith,' he said, 'why did you doubt?'" (14:29-31).

Some might say that Peter's faith failed because he doubted and sank. However, our ideas of success and failure may not be the same as the Lord's. After all, Jesus favored the mite-giving widow over the religious elite. Peter may have failed in the eyes of others, but through trusting Jesus he was the only one who experienced walking on water. Granted, he did waver in his trust and sink, but he also felt Jesus lift him up. When Peter began to sink, he cried out, "Lord, save me!" At Peter's weakest moment he still trusted God to save him. And our faithful God did.

Peter trusted Jesus and took a leap of faith. As a result he experienced a grand adventure with Jesus. The other disciples missed out on that adventure. They didn't learn the valuable lesson of trusting Jesus the way Peter did that day because they weren't willing to take the leap.

At the heart of control is distrust—a distrust in God's sovereignty. God is in control whether we believe it or not, but we still have a decision to make. We can place our trust in ourselves or we can place our trust in the Creator of the universe. Solomon addressed this choice. "Those who trust in themselves are fools, but those who walk in wisdom are kept safe" (Prov. 28:26). This isn't to say that God's plan doesn't include painful experiences. Heartache will come, but the strength and help of the Lord comes to those who put their trust in him. "The LORD is my strength and my shield; my heart trusts in him, and he helps me" (Ps. 28:7). Trusting in God's sovereignty is a leap of faith. We can be confident that it is a leap that leads to the grandest of spiritual adventures.

The Impatient Serial Sinner

and the Patient Grace of God

It was one of those days. Everything had gone wrong. I had accidentally set the alarm clock to p.m. rather than a.m., the dog had accidentally wet the bed—our bed—and the kids had accidentally forgotten to eat their granola bars as they rushed to get in the car. Everyone's "accidents" caused my temper teapot to begin simmering before eight o'clock. Slowly, the events of the morning started to agitate and boil, until finally a lot of noise escaped from the little hole in the top of my kettle. In other words, I blew my top.

I ranted all the way through the drive-through. Then I raved when my daughter dropped her iced cini-minis among all the dirt that had accumulated during six months of not vacuuming the car. *A little dirt never hurt anyone*, I had previously reasoned with myself. The low gas light was blinking and we had *minus* ten minutes to be at the orthodontist. Who needed gas when the fumes *I* was giving off were good for at least another fifteen miles?

I turned onto the interstate, which of course was limited to one driving lane due to road construction. Then I stomped on the accelerator, taking us from zero to seventy in point-two seconds. Reaching my desired speed (you don't want to know), I set the cruise control and popped a tater tot into my mouth. Suddenly, I had to slam on the brakes and resume a much slower speed behind a car that appeared to be an early 1940s model. I've always been an impatient driver, verbally labeling anyone going slower than me a moron, and anyone going faster than me an idiot. Whoever was driving this should-be-retired blast from the past was redefining my idea of moron.

"Isn't there a law against driving too slow?" I slurped my coffee and complained to my children. My daughter Alex, who was seven at the time, asked, "Mom, is there really a law against going too slow?"

"Yes, sweetie, I believe there is, and if I were a police officer I'd throw this moron in jail and have that fossil he's driving impounded!" I shot back through clenched teeth. "This is ridiculous!" I yelled. "We could get out and walk faster than this! This man obviously doesn't have a life. Am I the only person in the world who has places to be? He's going to get someone killed driving this slow!"

Making an unwise decision based on my impatience, I swerved onto the right-hand shoulder and proceeded to pass moron-man, who was making us late for the orthodontist appointment. Meanwhile Alex, who had watched way too many episodes of Andy Griffith and had proclaimed Barney Fife and Gomer Pyle her childhood heroes, rolled down the window and started yelling at the elderly, wide-eyed driver, "Citizen's arrest! Citizen's arrest!"

I'm not sure if the worst part of the ordeal was the example I set for my children that day or the glorious view of the "Jesus Loves You" bumper sticker I provided for the elderly driver as we smoked past him.

Impatient Serial Sinner: One who places her high-strung, irritable, anxious, agitated, short-tempered, rude temperament and agenda above the feelings and well-being of another.

The Patient Grace of God

Throughout biblical history, Jesus was constantly faced with circumstances that could have prompted him to lose it with people, particularly his own disciples. The very ones who were chosen and privileged to walk with the Creator of the universe constantly tried his patience with their complaining, lack of faith, and self-seeking egos. I can just see them walking with Jesus on the dusty road to Capernaum, pushing one another and arguing like a bunch of ten-year-old boys over who was greatest (Mark 9:34). When they stopped to rest, Jesus told them about how the first would be last and the last would be first, but it went in one ear and out the other.

On their way to Jerusalem, James and John started again. They even had the audacity to ask the King of kings to share his glory with them: "Then James and John, sons of Zebedee, came to him. 'Teacher,' they said, 'we want you to do for us whatever we ask. . . . Let one of us sit at your right and the other at your left in your glory'" (Mark 10:35, 37). Can you believe the nerve of some people? How I admire the patience of Christ as he calmly explained that the seats of honor in the heavenly realm didn't belong to them.

The disciples also tested Christ's patience with their constant misunderstandings of his teachings. Jesus offered an amazing illustration in his parable of the sower, and the dumbfounded disciples were clueless. They were probably too busy arguing over who would have the biggest garden on Paradise Street to pay attention. You can almost hear the concern in his voice as Jesus responded to their lack of understanding, "Don't you understand this parable? How then will you understand any parable?" (Mark 4:13).

Another test of Jesus' patience with his disciples came in putting up with their lack of faith. Peter eagerly hopped out of the boat to walk on water, only to falter in faith and sink (Matt. 14:29-30). A lack of faith hindered the disciples from casting out demons in Jesus' name (Matt. 17:14-21). It's hard for us not to picture Jesus throwing up his hands as he responded, "You unbelieving and perverse generation . . . how long shall I stay with you? How long shall I put up with you?" (Matt. 17:17). But rather than throwing in the towel and hitching a cloud ride back to heaven, he patiently remained on earth to fulfill the will of the Father.

The disciples could not have become the faithful servants of God they later came to be without the endurance and patience of Christ. And while the disciples were in desperate need of God's endurance, our own hope, salvation, and service to him are no less dependent upon his patience.

There are many examples of God choosing patience over wrath with people of wavering faith. The "stiff-necked" Israelites provide one such example. God tolerated the whining and complaining of the Israelites through forty years in the wilderness. He could have gotten tired of their griping and wiped them out with the blink of an eye. Yet, we are told, "for about forty years he endured their conduct in the wilderness" (Acts 13:18). God was patient with this stubborn, hard-hearted generation for many years.

I can't imagine how God remained patient with Israel. Theirs was a spineless faith from the get-go. As they were miraculously escaping Egypt, they became trapped between the murderous Egyptian army and the Red Sea. Suddenly, their celebration parade ceased, they dropped their frankincense, and their eyeballs came out on stems. All of the miracles God had performed became hazy, and their blissful chant of "Hip, Hip, Hooray!" was replaced with faithless complaining. "Didn't we say to you in Egypt, 'Leave us alone; let us serve the Egyptians'? It would have been better for us to serve the Egyptians than to die in the desert!" (Ex. 14:12). Had I been God, I would have said, "No, it would be better for you to die in the desert!" Then I would have whipped up an extra salty tidal wave and wiped 'em all out. *Whoooosh!* Lucky for us all, I'm not God. Our faithful God patiently endured the contempt of his terrified people, and once again delivered them from their enemies.

There was also a time when the Israelites fashioned an idol and credited it with God's act of deliverance saying, "These are your gods, Israel, who brought you up out of Egypt" (Ex. 32:4). How soon they forgot! God's anger burned against them and about 3000 of them died, but in his patience he didn't destroy the nation.

Again and again, the Israelites tested God's patience, and every time the Lord endured their insults, faithlessness, and rejection. Psalm 78 tells us, "Yet he was merciful; he forgave their iniquities and did not destroy them. Time after time he restrained his anger and did not stir up his full wrath" (v. 38).

Certainly, the Israelites faced consequences. Because of rebelling against God's commands, murmuring, forsaking God, and worshiping idols, they suffered hardships including exiles and captivities.

Consequences do not happen *instead* of God's patience; they happen *in light of* God's patience. They are part of his perfect plan for maturing us and making us more like him.

God Calls Christians to Patience

While you may have chuckled at my impatience at the beginning of this chapter, most of us have experienced an aggravation toward others while driving. Road rage is serious business these days. BBC News reported a study of drivers aged sixteen to thirty in the United Kingdom. The results were startling. While 20 percent reported encountering road rage in other drivers more than ten times, more than 70 percent admitted succumbing to road rage themselves.[3] Newton Hightower quoted the *New York Times* in his article entitled, "The Startling Statistics on Road Rage." "A recent Gallup poll reported that motorists were more worried about road rage (42 percent) than about drunk driving (35 percent)."[4] Angry, impatient drivers are becoming a major problem in our country. Americans are in too big of a hurry.

How about waiting in a long line at a supermarket? Honestly, I can't stand it. I always think the line next to me is moving faster, so I switch. Sure enough, as soon as I do, the check-out lady in my new line speaks into her microphone in a drawn-out, depressing tone, "I need a price check at register nine."

How about automated telephone menus? "Please listen carefully as our menu options have changed. If you are calling about this, press one. If you are calling about that, press two. To hear this menu in Spanish, press *numero tres*." Ten minutes and eight eyeball rolls later the automated voice says, "To hear this menu again, press eighty-four." When you finally get a live person on the line and explain the reason for your call, she says, "Oh, you need to talk to so-and-so. Please hold." Then another menu begins—or worse, you are suddenly disconnected and must call back to start the fun all over again.

What triggers your impatience? Is it slow-moving lines? Is it the ever-annoying telemarketers who call during dinner or your favorite television show? Is it drivers who seem to have acquired a license from a shady character on the street with a long black coat? No matter what ruffles your feathers, God can use it to work his patience into your life.

Knowing that impatience often flares in our dealings with one another, God inspired Paul to write about how the two relate. In Ephesians 4:2 he writes, "Be patient, bearing with one another in love." Other verses reiterate God's command for Christians to be patient, citing patience as a way to calm a quarrel (Prov. 15:18) and show love towards others (1 Cor. 13:4). For many of us, quarrel-calming is a tool that could use sharpening. A little patience can keep us the sharpest knife in the kitchen!

I have to admit that my challenging you to be patient is the pot calling the kettle black. While writing this chapter I came upon Matthew 7:3-5, the verses that tell me not to remove the speck from my brother's eye before removing the plank from my own, and I feared that God was going to strike me with a lightning bolt! When I told a family member the theme of this book, he said while chuckling, "Well, I hope chapter 1 is on patience." With all the shock I could muster, I replied, "Are you referring to *moi*?"

I'll never forget riding with my dad to the grocery store a couple of years back. Talk about a slow driver! My dad is one of those drivers who trigger road rage in other people. However, if they only knew the unselfish things he does for their benefit, they would applaud him rather than calling him number one (with the wrong finger).

Daddy and I had been circling the parking lot for several minutes looking for a place to park. Suddenly, I spotted a car pulling out of a space near the front of the store, on the next aisle over. "Hurry up, Daddy! If you'll floor it we might be able to beat everyone over there!" I don't believe "flooring it" is in the man's vocabulary. With me drumming my fingers on my knee and trying to hold my tongue, he slowly meandered his way over to the next aisle. The car crept up to the spot, and I began to unbuckle my seatbelt, preparing to make a mad dash to the entrance. Much to my dismay, he passed the parking spot. "Daddy! What are you doing?" I whined.

"Well, there's an elderly lady in the car behind us and I thought I'd let her have that space," he smiled.

"You *what?*" I erupted! "Nobody thinks like that! There is no way that lady would have done that for you! Besides, don't you know that walking is good for elderly people?" I huffed.

While I couldn't believe Daddy would give up our rightful spot for a stranger and make his only daughter walk *all the way* from the back of the lot, it did inspire me to think. I concluded that he had set a great example of being patient for the benefit of someone else. Jesus said that when we do something good in order to be recognized by others, we have received our reward in full, but when we do it in secret for the benefit of others and the glory of God, great is our reward in heaven. I can imagine Daddy and me in heaven, with him receiving his beautiful, well-jeweled crown as I stand impatiently in the back of the line . . . drumming my fingers.

What about standing in those long lines? Those moments are perfect opportunities to "be still and know that he is God." Rather than line-hopping, perhaps taking a moment to fellowship with Jesus would serve us better. Or we could acknowledge the person behind us and ask about his day. Too often our impatience overshadows opportunities to invest time in blessing other people. I can safely say that impatience is the work of the Enemy, probably in more ways than we know. Being patient and taking time to consider the needs and feelings of those around us is a powerful way to bless others and bring glory to God.

Perhaps the patience pill I find hardest to swallow comes when I witness those who succeed in schemes that hurt others yet seem to face no consequences for their actions. Some people thrive on deceiving and plotting against others for their own gratification and personal gain. Some are even heavily involved in the church to disguise who they really are while they feed on trusting, grace-driven Christians. The church is their breeding ground, offering them a mask of Christianity and a slew of unsuspecting believers of whom they take advantage. Through an abuse of grace, they prey and use, leaving hurting victims in their wake of devastation. Of these people the Scriptures warn, "For certain individuals whose condemnation was written about long ago have secretly slipped in among you. They are ungodly people, who pervert the grace of our God into a license for immorality . . ." (Jude 4).

It is hard to be patient when it comes to these godless people who continuously harm others. We ask, "God, why do you allow them to prosper? Why did you allow so-and-so, who did so much good for your glory, to die young while allowing this godless man, who does nothing but harm your people, to go on living? How is this fair? How is this just? How is this right? Why, God, why?" The truth is, we can't know why. We can't fully comprehend the wisdom and purpose of God. But we can know that he is a just and righteous God. We can trust that his ways are perfect and his plan is for the good of those who love him. What doesn't make sense to us does make sense to God. In the Psalms, we are encouraged not to fret and to be patient as we wait on God. "Be still before the LORD and wait patiently for him; do not fret when people succeed in their ways, when they carry out their wicked schemes" (Ps. 37:7). We can rest in the assurance that God is just.

People of malicious intent, who cruelly bring harm to others for selfish gain, may not receive their just penalty according to our timing, but they will in God's. Peter assures us, "They will be paid back with harm for the harm they have done" (2 Peter 2:13). Those who take pleasure in evil will most certainly come to justice. In the meantime, in our patience, we must forgive. Forgiveness doesn't always mean to trust someone again. In fact, the Scriptures give instructions for dealing with the godless people who have secretly slipped in among us. We are to forgive, but we are also wisely instructed to "have nothing to do with such people" (2 Tim. 3:5).

For some, the forgiveness part is hard. Certainly, our forgiveness is for the glory of God and a command to be followed, but it is to our benefit as well. When we truly forgive and let go of wrongs done to us or to those we love, we are happier because we are not living in the bondage of anger and bitterness. Miserable are those who demand God's immediate justice for those who do wrong. The righteous justice of God is not within our control. When we let go of trying to control justice and questioning God's methods, those chains of bondage are broken and we are set free.

It is also not within our power to understand the miserable bondage in which a godless person is enslaved. I often wonder if a large measure of God's justice is already being poured out in the hearts of the wicked. As they go about their lives of deceit, inflicting pain on others, it may seem that they are prospering and getting away with it, but we cannot know the inner turmoil they are in as a result of their wrongful choices. We are created for the purpose of bringing glory to God. Therefore, when individuals are not bringing glory to God, they are not fulfilling their purpose. This lack of fulfillment would have to bring about a miserably unsatisfying striving for happiness and contentment, which cannot be achieved apart from knowing and loving God.

Jesus exemplified what it means to be patient with people. So are we to work harder to demonstrate that same patience with others, no matter how ignorant, arrogant, or undeserving they might be? Certainly not in our own strength. Instead, we must recognize that patience cannot be achieved through our own efforts, but through abiding in the patience of Christ.

We cannot produce the fruit of patience apart from Christ. Jesus revealed this truth in the gospel of John when he said, "I am the vine; you are the branches. If you remain in me and I in you, you will bear much fruit; apart from me you can do nothing" (15:5). We grow God's fruit not when we try harder, but when we seek life from the Vine. Our fruit dies along with our efforts unless we stay connected to the Source. The vine is the life-source of the branches. Every fruit produced by the branches originates from and is sustained by the vine. We can do nothing on our own, but we are strengthened, effective, and productive through the power of Jesus Christ, in whom we live. Therefore, since God is patient we radiate patience.

In the same way that we rely upon God's patience with us, let us also rely on the indwelling Holy Spirit to manifest his patience through us toward others. It's all about the Vine and the branches.

5

The Miserly Serial Sinner

and the Generous Grace of God

While I consistently throw everything out now, I was a miserly child. I never threw anything away. I remember saving candy in elementary school. My brother and I got candy in our baskets on Easter morning, our stockings on Christmas Eve, and our pumpkins on Halloween night. Then there were those occasions when our granddad would give us each a dollar and take us to the Zippy Mart down the street from our house. Back in the 1970s you could fill a whole bag with candy for a dollar. While my brother would devour his candy the minute he got it (the pig!), I proudly kept mine hidden in a box under my bed.

I wouldn't eat it because then I wouldn't have any more. I wouldn't show it to anyone because they might ask for a piece, and then I wouldn't have the abundance I treasured. I wouldn't share it with my younger brother who coveted it because the thought of him gobbling up all of his own candy and then conning me out of mine just didn't sit right with me. So what did I do with it? I just kept it. Sometimes, in the privacy of my room, I would pull it out, look at it, and think, *Wow, I really have a lot of candy!* My mouth would water as I grabbed huge handfuls and watched it pour like rain from my hands back into the box. Eventually, it got so old and nasty looking that my mom insisted I throw it away.

I also saved crab shells from restaurants. Don't ask why. I don't know why. It was a smelly collection. While I was growing up, our family loved to eat seafood. My favorite item on the menu was stuffed crab. I would eat the delicious stuffing out of the shell, wrap the shell in a napkin, take it home, and add it to the crab collection box under my bed. After a few months of collecting, the odor would become so disgusting that my mom would throw those out too.

Some of us hoard God's love, keeping it to ourselves rather than sharing it with others. We are thankful we have a Savior, gladly accepting all he wants to give us. We enjoy his comfort when we are sad, his assurance when we are uncertain, and his provision when we are in need. We bask in his goodness, mercy, and grace. Yet we keep all of those blessings in a box, tucked safely away in our hearts. We keep him a secret and enjoy him only in private. After all, someone else might not understand what we see in him.

Sometimes there's an urge to share the treasure of Christ, and we consider opening the box in our hearts to let someone peek inside. We know that they could "taste and see that the Lord is good," but what if they don't bite? What if their appetite isn't the same as ours? What if they don't appreciate the treasure we offer? What if they decide the Christ we crave isn't what they hunger for? Too often those "what if" fears keep us from sharing with others the treasure we have in Christ.

Other things Christians might hoard include money and possessions. I was once close to an elderly couple who hoarded money and material things. Part of the reason was the mentality they had derived from living through the Great Depression. It was an awful economic time for people. Banks closed, people lost their jobs, the stock market crashed, and people's money had little to no value. Food was rationed and people had to make do with what little they had. As they suffered through years of poor economic conditions, people hoarded everything. Many never got over it.

This couple saved everything. They saved empty ice cream buckets, butter tubs, and paper sacks. They saved worn-out clothes, twist ties from bread packaging, boxes, and bottles. They even saved broken lamps, torn sheets, and styrofoam meat trays. They saved everything from A to Z that could possibly be reused in any way.

The stockpiled "treasures" grew into large mounds, resulting in the need to purchase a storage shed. The treasures were never used, only saved. Sadly, as the years went by, the obsession to save both money and things grew into a terrible bondage of fear and worry in the hearts of this couple. Fear that future needs could only be met by hoarding. Worry that they might not have enough to ensure their own happiness. The more they saved, the further they sank into the bondage of *needing* to save. We are forewarned to avoid this snare in Ecclesiastes: "Whoever loves money never has enough; whoever loves wealth is never satisfied with their income. This too is meaningless" (5:10). We are also told how pointless it is to hoard things. "As goods increase, so do those who consume them. And what benefit are they to the owner except to feast their eyes on them?" (5:11).

During the wife's last years, the house would get unbearably hot. Alabama heat has claimed the lives of many elderly people. But no matter how hot it got, they would only use one small window air conditioner in the family room, and only during the day. They tolerated the night heat with no air-conditioning at all. The wife, especially, suffered in the horrendous heat day after day, senselessly risking heatstroke, while they hoarded hundreds of thousands of dollars in the bank.

I understand that some families can't afford to run air-conditioning, and many people in other countries don't even have the option. However, when God blesses us with a material thing, it brings him honor when we thankfully accept it, enjoy it, use it to bless others, and praise him for it. We are encouraged in Ecclesiastes, "When God gives someone wealth and possessions, and the ability to enjoy them, to accept their lot and be happy in their toil—this is a gift of God" (5:19). He is the Giver of all good things. Certainly, it honors God to be good stewards and not be wasteful. It is not sinful to use air-conditioning conservatively. However, it is sinful to hoard treasures on earth for reasons of fear, worry, or selfish gain.

It was heartbreaking to witness the way the vice of hoarding crushed this couple's morale and impaired their vision to see God's faithfulness. Not only did they miss out on the blessings of enjoying God's provisions, but also on the blessings of sharing God's provisions with others.

When it was all said and done, the day came for the shed to be cleared. As we helped throw away all the ruined, useless things that moth and rust had destroyed, God's Word rang true. We are not to store up for ourselves "treasures on earth," but "treasures in heaven" (Matt. 6:19-20).

God's spiritual blessings are for us to enjoy, share, and use for his glory, rather than hoard. The Bible says we are blessed with peace. "[T]he Lord blesses his people with peace" (Ps. 29:11). What peace there is in God's provisions! We can count on him to provide us with "everything we need for a godly life" (2 Peter 1:3). He gives us what we need, and many times even more than we need. There's no peace when we hoard his blessings, living in fear of losing them. We are to live confidently and expectantly in Christ, rejoicing in his provisions for us, no matter how big or small.

The Israelites hoarded God's manna. Traveling through the desert, the Israelites grew hungry. God poured manna from heaven, providing them with physical nutrition (Ex. 16:14-18). Through Moses, God instructed them to eat their fill but not to save any. God wanted them to trust him to provide daily food, rather than to greedily store it up for later, but the Israelites didn't obey. Exodus 16:20 tells us, "However, some of them paid no attention to Moses; they kept part of it until morning, but it was full of maggots and began to smell." Their hoarding did not result in physical gain and they also lost the joy of God's blessing by trusting in themselves rather than him.

God is the great Provider. There is no need to hoard and be miserly. He has generously clothed us, fed us, and given us all that we need. Jesus reminds us that the lilies do not labor or spin, but they are clothed in his splendor. He adds, "If that is how God clothes the grass of the field, which is here today, and tomorrow is thrown into the fire, how much more will he clothe you—you of little faith!" (Luke 12:27-28).

Remember the Y2K scare about computers not being able to roll over from the year 1999 to the year 2000? Many panicked, storing up food and other necessities. Our family didn't exactly panic, but we did think it wise to make a few preparations *just in case*. Okay, well, maybe we panicked a little. (We laugh together about this.) We cleaned out and designated an entire walk-in closet to prepare for the inevitable Y2K disaster that was sure to strike and leave us all to starve to death. I don't know about food, but we sure had enough coffee filters! We finished using up our stash in 2007! I grinned when I purchased our first package of filters after seven years. I don't know what we were thinking. We must have had a thousand coffee filters.

Jesus tells us not to worry about such things. "And do not set your heart on what you will eat or drink; do not worry about it. For the pagan world runs after all such things, and your Father knows that you need them" (Luke 12:29-30). How do we not worry, though? It's human nature to worry about such things. However, God says that all we have to do is seek him. When we live in his power and hope, worries dissipate and provisions come. Again, he is the great Provider. "But seek first his kingdom and his righteousness, and all these things will be given to you as well. Therefore do not worry about tomorrow, for tomorrow will worry about itself. Each day has enough trouble of its own" (Matt. 6:33-34). When we live in him, we don't have to worry. All that we need is found in the Bread of Life, the Living Water—Jesus Christ.

Miserly Serial Sinner: *One who is tightfisted and stingy, obtaining an unsatisfying pleasure in acquiring and hoarding money, possessions, or spiritual wisdom to the detriment of blessing others and glorifying God.*

The Generous Grace of God

Our Father in heaven holds nothing back when it comes to generosity. He created the amazing world in which we live, giving us rich land and water, plants and trees that bear nutritious vegetables and delicious fruit, greater light for the days and lesser light for the nights.

He even pleasures our taste buds with seafood, cheeseburgers, and country fried chicken! God said that all of these blessings were created for us. "'Rule over the fish of the sea and the birds of the air and over every living creature that moves on the ground.' Then God said, 'I give you every seed-bearing plant on the face of the whole earth and every tree that has fruit with seed in it. They will be yours for food'" (Gen. 1:28-29).

God generously gives his comfort when we need it. My friend Marlo lost her first husband in a plane crash. From the moment they married she feared losing him to death as a result of his dangerous military missions. Fear paralyzed her every time he went out on a job, forgot to check in when he said he would, or was late getting home. Although his death was her worst nightmare come true, this amazing young widow and mother of an adorable five-year-old son clung to Jesus and begged for his comfort, which he faithfully provided. God comforted this widow with a peace that passes understanding. Now God uses Marlo to bestow the same comfort she received on others who are walking through the devastating grief of losing a loved one.

King David understood and expressed the depth of God's comfort. "Even though I walk through the darkest valley, I will fear no evil, for you are with me; your rod and your staff, they comfort me" (Ps. 23:4). Just as God comforted David when he feared for his life and Marlo after she lost her husband, he also comforts us when we need it. God said through the prophet Jeremiah, "I will give them comfort and joy instead of sorrow" (31:13).

Not only does he comfort us but, out of his great love for us, he also shares in our sufferings. He doesn't just ride in and save the day with his comfort as a God who doesn't relate to or feel for his children. He actually suffered for us, and now he continues to sympathize with us and intercedes for us. The more we die to our own hurts and suffering—the more he lives through us—the more we are enabled to fully receive his comfort. Paul confirms this in 2 Corinthians 1:5: "For just as we share abundantly in the sufferings of Christ, so also our comfort abounds through Christ."

God gives his strength when we are weak. Check out Psalm 29:11: "The LORD gives strength to his people." We can delight in our weaknesses because the weaker we are, the more generously God gives his strength. Therefore, we can delight in Christ when we are insulted, persecuted, or made to feel useless. We can delight in Christ when we face financial hardships. We can delight in Christ when life throws us a curveball and we face all kinds of difficulties. It's through our weaknesses that God's strength is made real in our lives. Paul put it like this: "That is why, for Christ's sake, I delight in weaknesses, in insults, in hardships, in persecutions, in difficulties. For when I am weak, then I am strong" (2 Cor. 12:10). The glory of God is shown as we die to our own weaknesses and live in the strength of Christ.

Although Jesus was, is, and will always be the King of kings, he came to generously serve those he loved, even to the point of giving his own life. Jesus said, "For even the Son of Man did not come to be served, but to serve, and to give his life as a ransom for many" (Mark 10:45). God generously gives many good things to his children. He gives peace: "Peace I leave with you; my peace I give you" (John 14:27). He gives joy when we remain in him: "If you keep my commands, you will remain in my love, just as I have kept my Father's commands and remain in his love. I have told you this so that my joy may be in you and that your joy may be complete" (John 15:10-11). He gives rich blessings to those who seek him: "[T]he same Lord is Lord of all and richly blesses all who call on him" (Rom. 10:12).

More than these wonderful physical and emotional blessings we enjoy, God gave us his Son as a ransom for our sinful spiritual condition. Remember John 3:16? "For God so loved the world that he gave his one and only Son, that whoever believes in him shall not perish but have eternal life." He also gives the gift of his Holy Spirit. "Peter replied, 'Repent and be baptized, every one of you, in the name of Jesus Christ for the forgiveness of your sins. And you will receive the gift of the Holy Spirit'" (Acts 2:38). A tremendous gift we have in the Holy Spirit is his counsel. "But the Advocate, the Holy Spirit, whom the Father will send in my name, will teach you all things and will remind you of everything I have said to you" (John 14:26).

God is the Giver of all things, generously providing us with his rich and marvelous physical and spiritual blessings. While these blessings are for us to enjoy, they are also for us to share and use for his glory.

God Calls Christians to Generosity

I was talking to a restaurant waitress the other day in my hometown. She was telling me how she loved to work on Friday and Saturday nights because the "drinkers" were so generous with tips. When I asked about tips during weeknights, I was saddened by her response. "Weeknights aren't nearly as bad as Sundays," she said. "One of our busiest rushes is when church lets out on Sunday. But I tell you, Christians are the stingiest customers we have." She went on to say that many of the "churchgoers" left less than a 10 percent tip and some left no tip at all.

She was really put out with one group of churchgoers who had eaten there the previous Sunday. Two waitresses hadn't shown up for work so everyone had to serve extra tables, and the kitchen was shorthanded with only one cook. She said, "I kindly explained to the church group that it might take longer than usual, but the people were rude and demanding. There was nothing I could do but apologize and try to keep up with all my tables." She went on to tell me that these people left her a one-dollar bill and a tract on "How to Become a Christian," which I'm sure she promptly threw in the trash.

I have been guilty of leaving a tip in accordance with service, but after listening to this young waitress, I have vowed to leave a generous tip no matter what the circumstances. If Jesus Christ can be so generous as to die for me, an undeserving sinner, the least I can do is leave a generous tip to a waitress or waiter who didn't earn it. Christ doesn't require us to work for his gift of grace; he freely gives it. It's a gift we don't deserve, not a wage we have earned. Stinginess comes from a person who is not living in the goodness of God. Generosity is what Christ does through us.

Some do not understand that giving comes from the heart, not the pocket. In other words, it doesn't matter if you can't give what the wealthy give. Generosity is not in the amount but the motive. Luke tells about the time Jesus was watching the wealthy put their gifts into the temple treasury. When the rich bigwigs had finished tossing weighty bags of wealth into the pot, a poor widow walked up and dropped two meager coins into the offering (probably wishing she had more to give). Jesus confirmed that the amount is not what matters most to him. "'Truly I tell you,' he said, 'this poor widow has put in more than all the others. All these people gave their gifts out of their wealth; but she out of her poverty put in all she had to live on'" (21:3-4). I'd be willing to bet ten weighty bags of gold that the poor widow was the one who went home with a heart full of joy that day.

Paul says that the motive behind generosity is more important to Christ than the amount. "For if the willingness is there, the gift is acceptable according to what one has, not according to what one does not have" (2 Cor. 8:12). Sometimes I wish I had a million dollars to give, but I have to remember that God doesn't want my money, he wants my heart. If I were dirt poor and could only give one dollar with a joyful heart, God would be no less pleased than if I'd given one million dollars. To take it a step further, he's more pleased with a dollar given with a joyful heart than with a million given begrudgingly.

Some of us are stingy with money. I can't tell you how many times I've seen people with poor hygiene and tattered clothes standing on the roadside with a sign announcing "I'm hungry" and judged them rather than helped them. I've been guilty of justifying my actions by convincing myself that they are without excuse for being hungry. "This is America," I'd mumble under my breath. "There are plenty of jobs available. You should be out looking for one instead of begging for food." I'd convince myself that they have chosen a life of poverty, refusing to help themselves, and thus are unworthy of my time or money. However, God has convicted me of this mentality. Who am I to judge who is worthy of help?

I am not a judge. I cannot know the hearts of man, only God can. My responsibility is to help those who are in need. If a man is standing in front of me saying he is hungry, who am I to determine whether or not he deserves my help? Even if I gave food to someone who didn't deserve it, Jesus taught that those who give to others are giving to him. When I get to heaven and stand before Jesus, I can't imagine him saying, "I'm very disappointed that you gave that man on the side of the road a hamburger."

While generosity toward the needy is good, we must also be wise stewards. Unfortunately, many people are homeless because an alcohol or drug addiction has dominated their lives. They may ask for money for food, but after they receive money, they spend it on the next hit or bottle of booze. We don't want to support an addiction so it's best to meet their need with food rather than cash.

Like my parents and brother, I used to own a restaurant. We had Bible verses on the walls and the parking lot marquee, which attracted people in need. Often we were asked to give money toward gas, or car repairs, or an electric bill. We learned quickly that it was wiser to call the owner of a gas station, auto repair shop, or electric company and pay with a credit card after service had been rendered than to hand out money. Many times the people in need never showed up at the gas station or repair shop because that's not really why they wanted money. That wasn't always the case, though. Often people were genuinely blessed by our willingness to help. The bottom line is that generosity is good, but it also calls for wisdom.

In the parable of the sheep and the goats, Jesus said, "For I was hungry and you gave me something to eat, I was thirsty and you gave me something to drink, I was a stranger and you invited me in, I needed clothes and you clothed me, I was sick and you looked after me, I was in prison and you came to visit me." Then the Bible says that the righteous will answer him, "Lord, when did we see you hungry and feed you, or thirsty and give you something to drink? When did we see you a stranger and invite you in, or needing clothes and clothe you? When did we see you sick or in prison and go to visit you?" Then Jesus will say, "Truly I tell you, whatever you did for one of the least of these brothers and sisters of mine, you did for me"(Matt. 25:35-40).

Jesus offers no measuring stick as to who is "the least of these" and who is not. He never warns about being too generous. He simply states that whatever we do for those in need, we do for him. Our focus shouldn't be on judging who is worthy and who is not, but on discovering "How can I serve God by serving the least of these?" When I zip through a drive-through and deliver hot food to a hungry person, I never regret it. It always gives me joy to help someone in need.

Of all the serial sinners in the Bible, I believe Paul took the cake. Before God changed his name to Paul, he was known as Saul. Saul did horrible things to people. He hated Christians and made every effort to destroy the church. He dragged men and women who professed faith in God from their homes and threw them in prison, and even went so far as to stand by giving his approval when Stephen, an innocent man, was stoned to death (Acts 8:1, 3). Saul was one bad dude.

But once Saul surrendered his life to Jesus (and was renamed Paul), he generously gave his time and money for the glory of God and the service of others. Many of us have given our hearts to Jesus as Paul did, but we struggle with giving our time, money, and service. Why is it that some people struggle while others find it easy to fully give of themselves?

We all know people, usually only one or two, who truly live self-sacrificing lives. They have devoted their hearts and minds to joyfully serving other people, humbly considering others better than themselves in word and action. They never complain or grumble about having to do something for someone else. They always seem to be available for those in need of help, counsel, or encouragement. If you did something sinful and wanted to talk to someone about it, you would seek out this person because you know he or she would not judge you. You would be confident that this person truly has your best interests at heart and would love you in spite of the terrible thing you had done.

Think about that person. What makes him or her and the apostle Paul so different from the average Christian? How can anyone be so generous with their time, money, and service to God and others? How do these types of people refrain from judging other people?

How do they show unconditional love to those who don't deserve it? How do they spend so little time thinking about themselves?

What about people who give away a lot of money? How do they give away what they could use for their own enjoyment for the sake of someone else, even someone they don't know? Those who are truly successful at being sacrificial don't do any of those things in their own strength.

Paul and those who freely give of themselves have learned the secret of the gospel, which is to die to self and live in Christ. Paul explained in Galatians 2:20-21. "I have been crucified with Christ and I no longer live, but Christ lives in me. The life I now live in the body, I live by faith in the Son of God, who loved me and gave himself for me. I do not set aside the grace of God, for if righteousness could be gained through the law, Christ died for nothing!" Paul is saying that if we could behave like Christians in our own strength, Christ died for nothing. Paul understood that the only way to live as Christ calls us to live is to live *in* Christ. That means dying to self and trusting Jesus to live through us.

It was easy for Paul to grasp this because God so radically saved and changed him from the horrible person he was. When we live for ourselves rather than the glory of God, we are miserable people. Paul went from living a miserably selfish life to being a man full of joy and hope. He was deeply appreciative to God, who taught him to die to his old self and to live in Christ. Here is what he said about it.

I thank Christ Jesus our Lord, who has given me strength, that he considered me trustworthy, appointing me to his service. Even though I was once a blasphemer and a persecutor and a violent man, I was shown mercy because I acted in ignorance and unbelief. The grace of our Lord was poured out on me abundantly, along with the faith and love that are in Christ Jesus.

Here is a trustworthy saying that deserves full acceptance: Christ Jesus came into the world to save sinners—of whom I am the worst. But for that very reason I was shown mercy so that in me, the worst of sinners, Christ Jesus might display his immense patience as an example for those who would believe in him and receive eternal life.

Now to the King eternal, immortal, invisible, the only God, be honor and glory for ever and ever. Amen. (1 Tim. 1:12-17).

We are a nation with plenty of resources but little time. It seems the more we know and the more we have, the busier we become. As we become more and more affluent, we give less and less of our time for the sake of others. But there is victory in the death and resurrection of Christ. We don't have to live hoarding money, possessions, and time. We serve a Savior who died for our past, present, and future sins. He has overcome our stingy, sinful natures. Even harder to accept at times are the "future sins" he has overcome for us. In other words, we are Christians, but we are sinning Christians. We will most definitely blow it, but Christ has covered even our future sins. Therefore, we are blameless through Jesus.

We can become people who generously and joyfully give, but only if we are willing to die to ourselves so that Christ lives through us. It is through the power of Christ working in us that we are able to die. Then, by that same power, Christ lives through us. It is all about the power of Christ working in us and through us. That was Paul's secret. That is the secret of people we admire for their generosity and goodness, and that is the secret God offers us. The power to be generous and good is found in dying to our stingy, self-seeking nature and living in the generosity and goodness of Jesus Christ our Lord.

The Selfish Serial Sinner

and the Serving Grace of God

In searching my heart for how selfishness manifests itself, I have made some disturbing discoveries. There are many ways selfishness rears its ugly head in my life, but I believe the most prominent among them is my unwillingness to give of my time. I have no problem writing a check for a quick donation, sending a card to a sick friend, dropping items off at the Salvation Army Thrift Store to help those less fortunate, or offering a gift certificate to a family in need. Serving others in ways that do not involve a lot of time is not a problem for me. It's the acts of service that take large blocks of time and pull me away from what I want to do that bring out my selfishness.

Take the Christmas season, for example. I hate shopping and despise having to dwell on which gifts to purchase. Interrupting my routine to shop for gifts and wrap them frustrates me to no end. Ebenezer Scrooge can't hold a candle to me. I would be perfectly happy to simply celebrate the birth of our Lord without exchanging gifts. Not because I don't enjoy receiving gifts or watching loved ones enjoy the gifts I give, but because preparation for gift-giving eats up so much time. Selfishly, I'd rather do something else.

Determined to find a better way to spend my time, one December I came up with the perfect solution to end my shopping frustrations. Shrink wrap. Allow me to explain how it works. You simply wrap the clear paper around an item, apply warm air from a hairdryer, and wait as the paper "shrinks" to wrap tightly and flawlessly around the item. With just a flick of the switch on my hairdryer, I could make used items appear new while cleaning out my closets and attic at the same time. "Ginger," I said to myself, "you have just revolutionized your holiday season!"

With newfound purpose and determination, I purchased a $4.99 roll of shrink wrap and climbed the attic stairs. Oh, the treasures I found! I gleefully ran from box to box as I talked out loud to myself: "The comedy video of Dennis Swanberg would be perfect for Grandma! Terri Blackstock's suspense book would be just right for my mother-in-law, and my brother would absolutely love the multi-size wrench set (a leftover wedding gift from 1991)!" If my arms weren't so short, I would have patted myself on the back. It was a brilliant plan . . . or so I thought.

On Christmas Day the glitz and glitter of the holiday season was in full swing. The stockings were hung by the chimney with care; the fragrances of warm cider, cinnamon, and pine permeated the air; and "Have Yourself a Merry Little Christmas" played softly in the background. Laughter echoed throughout the living room and hugs were exchanged as we opened our gifts. A twinge of guilt tugged at my heart as I thought, *Should I feel bad for passing off used items as new? Nah, what better gifts than ones I have personally tested and approved?* I convinced myself I had chosen the perfect gifts.

I almost pulled it off, when suddenly my selfishness backfired. My mother-in-law opened the cover of her suspense book. "Hey!" she called out, "This book is signed 'To Ginger, from Dad!'" The music stopped, and the room grew uncomfortably quiet. A ball fell off the tree. So much for my brilliant plan.

Selfish Serial Sinner: *One who pursues the advancement of his or her own interests by focusing on and catering to his or her own feelings, happiness, importance, and well-being while disregarding the best interests of others.*

The Serving Grace of God

Throughout his earthly ministry, Jesus did not serve himself. He served his Father and, in turn, he served others. He did not let the opinions of others or the ideals of good time management dictate his days. Instead, he concerned himself with doing the will of his Father and using as much time as needed to serve others, even when it only benefited one person.

As Jesus grew in popularity, he was in high demand. The disciples constantly urged him to minister only to large groups. I am confident that if the disciples had lived today, they would have authored and published *The Busy Savior's Guide to Time Management*.

The disciples did not understand why Jesus would waste time on one person. At one point Jesus was ministering to a large crowd when a sick woman who desired healing touched the edge of his cloak. Jesus stopped to acknowledge her faith by asking, "Who touched me?" Thinking in terms of the large number of people present, Peter said to Jesus, "Master, the people are crowding and pressing against you" (Luke 8:45). Peter knew it could have been anyone who touched the cloak of Jesus, and he probably thought it was silly to pause and single out just one person. Why spend time ministering to only one when there are so many? Yet that one woman was important to Jesus.

There were other times when Jesus took time to serve and the disciples thought it a waste of time. On one occasion Jesus was serving a large crowd in Judea by teaching and healing. The disciples were all about large crowds, but when children were brought to the scene and Jesus was asked to take time for them, the disciples viewed it as a mere distraction. They rebuked those who brought the children. But Jesus had other plans. He was about his Father's business, and his Father's business involved taking time to pray for and teach children (Matt. 19:13-14).

After Jesus had ministered in Judea, he began making his way back to Galilee. In order to get there, the Scriptures say "he had to go through Samaria" (John 4:4). What did it mean that he *had* to go through Samaria? Jesus actually had three options for mapping his journey. He could have followed the coast (which is still an operational route today), gone through Peraea (east of the Jordan River), or gone through Samaria. Had the disciples weighed in on the decision, going through Samaria surely would have been their last choice. Although traveling through Samaria was the most direct route, they would have avoided it like the plague. Jews simply did not associate with Samaritans. Yet Jesus *had* to go through Samaria. Was this because there were thousands waiting to hear his teaching and in need of his healing services? No. Jesus ignored the politically correct social ethics and shunned advised time management skills in order to minister to one woman. He *had* to go through Samaria because he had to do his Father's will by serving this woman.

The one woman for whom Jesus went through Samaria wasn't of value in the eyes of others. She was not even of value among her own people. She had had five husbands and had not married the sixth man with whom she was involved. (Once upon a time this was actually considered immoral.) Jesus, being the gracious, saving Lord that he is, took the time to reveal this woman's sins and explain her need for salvation.

When the disciples rejoined Jesus, they "were surprised to find him talking with a woman" (John 4:27). Not only were Jews and Samaritans forbidden to talk, but the normal prejudices of that time prohibited public communication between men and women in general. The fact that they were strangers only added to the impropriety. These man-made laws and rules didn't matter one iota to Jesus. All that mattered was the will of his Father, which entailed taking the time to offer one Samaritan woman the gift of eternal life.

Jesus intended his life on earth to be an example of purpose and practical application of service. He challenged us to live as he lived—the life of a servant. He said that whoever wanted to be served should serve, and whoever wanted to be first should be last (Mark 9:35). He set the example saying, "[T]he Son of Man did not come to be served but to serve, and to give his life as a ransom for many" (Matt. 20:28).

It has become our custom to do away with serving others. I remember when I could drive up to a "service station," now commonly referred to as a self-serve gas station, and a cheerful man with a kind smile would fill my tank, check my oil, and wash my windows. Now you don't have to interact with another human to purchase gasoline unless you live in Oregon or New Jersey. In most states, customer service has been replaced with self-service and pay-at-the-pump stations.

It's the same in many stores. Rather than a friendly face ringing up and bagging merchandise, we have the option of self-check. In the near future it is sure to be the only option. I avoided self-checkout counters at first. They were foreign. They looked complicated. They intimidated me. I just knew that if I attempted to operate one of those contraptions and tried to exit the store, sirens and alarms would go off. Cops would come running from all directions, and the SWAT team would rappel from the ceiling to tackle me. What happened to good old customer service? Service with a smile? We are slowly becoming a self-serving nation in more ways than one.

Jesus was not self-serving. His whole ministry from birth to death to resurrection was for the purpose of serving his Father's will. Although God the Father placed all things under the reign of the Son (1 Cor. 15:27-28), Jesus selflessly placed his very existence in the hands of his Father. He always sought his Father's will above his own agenda. Jesus said, "I seek not to please myself but him who sent me" (John 5:30). Perhaps the hardest time for him to do this was in Gethsemane just before his death. Jesus knew that his hour had come. He knew that he was about to be betrayed into the hands of those who would crucify him. With a heart that was overwhelmed with sorrow, Jesus cried out to his Father, "My Father, if it is possible, may this cup [of suffering and death] be taken from me. Yet not as I will, but as you will." After praying, he returned to check on his disciples, then went away a second time to pray, "My Father, if it is not possible for this cup to be taken away unless I drink it, may your will be done" (Matt. 26:39, 42). Jesus laid down his own agenda, his own preference, and his own life to obey his Father's will and serve mankind.

Jesus "made himself nothing, taking the very nature of a servant, being made in human likeness. And being found in appearance as a man, he humbled himself and became obedient to death—even death on a cross!" (Phil. 2:7-8). His death was his ultimate act of service. It was all for us. Isaiah records, "But he was pierced for our transgressions, he was crushed for our iniquities; the punishment that brought us peace was on him, and by his wounds we are healed" (53:5).

When it came to serving others; time, social trends, and personal agenda did not determine to whom Jesus would minister. He freely gave of himself for the service of all.

God Calls Christians to Serve

God calls Christians to serve, but it is contrary to the sinful nature. Self-preservation is naturally high on our priority list, inclining us to do whatever it takes to keep ourselves in good standing. To serve is to look to the best interest of another rather than gratifying our own need to be right, gain the upper hand, or secure a desired status. Selfishness always tries to benefit itself and always at the expense of others.

For example, in the midst of a marital argument a self-serving spouse refuses to admit fault, fights to be heard, and demands to be agreed with, while a spouse with a servant's heart disregards the fault of the other, recognizes his or her own fault, seeks forgiveness when necessary, and shows respect for a differing opinion. Another selfish response is to adopt a martyr mentality as a means of saving face and preserving dignity. Allow me to set up a scenario to demonstrate how a martyr mentality can develop as a result of a marital disagreement and see if you can relate.

Samantha and Bob are in the car. They've just disagreed over an issue. This issue is a hill on which Samantha is willing to die, so she is angry that Bob doesn't see things the way she does. Rather than respecting the fact that Bob is a unique creation of God with his own personality, thoughts, ideas, and opinions, Samantha selfishly fumes that Bob does not agree with her. Instead of focusing on the topic of discussion and devising a plan that might integrate strong points from both sides, she manipulates the situation by internalizing the argument. She refuses to continue respectfully working through the heart of the disagreement and instead deems her husband's difference of opinion a personal attack on her character.

Because she is focusing on herself not on the topic of disagreement she concludes that Bob has hurt her feelings. After all, isn't that what's most important? Doesn't the whole world revolve around a wife's feelings, happiness, and well-being? Doesn't she deserve to be doted on, respected above all else (especially in petty arguments), and placed on a pedestal? As she focuses on herself, she is convinced that Bob disagreeing with her infallible opinion just isn't acceptable. This isn't the life she signed up for. When she said "I do" what she really meant was "I *do* agree that you shall love, honor, and respect me above yourself. I *do* agree that my opinion is gold and the way my brain works is superior to the way your brain works. I'm always right about everything, and in time I *do* believe you will come to realize that."

By internalizing the focus and making it all about herself, Samantha embraces the martyr mentality. She is the wounded victim. Bob has hurt her feelings so badly, but for his sake, she turns her head so that he doesn't see her cry. In reality, she wants him to take note that she is crying and to praise her for selflessly trying to spare him from seeing that her feelings are hurt. Because she is selfishly internalizing the issue, she is playing games with herself and her husband. She stares out the window and pretends to be enamored with the scenery whizzing by. She thinks, *Soon he will come to admire the quiet, submissive wife that I am, realize what an inconsiderate jerk he is, and beg my forgiveness. If he really cares he will pull the car over, gently turn my tear-stained face to his, and be overcome with grief that he has upset me.*

Shouldn't my feelings be more important than a minor disagreement? she continues to reason in her head. Apparently not! After thirty minutes Samantha is still staring out the window and Bob has not confessed. At this point, Samantha's head is turned so far away from him that she is almost looking in the backseat. Her neck hurts. Bob really needs to confess before there is permanent muscle damage. *How can he continue driving while I am obviously distraught?* She inwardly moans. *Okay, I know that man is not reaching to turn on the radio. What, is he humming now? Oh . . . no! He is! He's humming! This is unbelievable! How can he hum when I'm upset? Doesn't he know that I'm only pretending not to be upset to protect his feelings because I am such a good wife? How dare he! Whatever happened to "as Christ loved the church and gave himself up for her?" Bob can't even give up the radio! Okay, calm down. This is how it must be. I must suck it up and live the life of a martyr now. I am a good wife, but I must carry on without the appreciation and affections of my husband who obviously doesn't love or respect me as he should.* This is the martyr mentality.

Unfortunately, I have fallen into the martyr mentality too many times. Of all the selfish intentions with which I struggle, the martyr mentality is probably the most cleverly disguised. I want my way—and I'm willing to give my husband the silent treatment to get it. However, if dissected with the scalpel of truth, it is the epitome of marital selfishness. Clamming up and proclaiming oneself a martyr as a response to a marital disagreement is nothing more than vain conceit. Paul warns, "Do nothing out of selfish ambition or vain conceit. Rather, in humility value others above yourselves" (Phil. 2:3). At the heart of deeming ourselves the "sacrificial victim" is pride. When we hide in a turtle shell of pride, unwilling to admit wrong or accept fault of any kind, we are looking to our own best interest. Paul goes on to warn that we should not be ". . . looking to [our] own interests but each of you to the interests of the others" (2:4).

To wholly serve another as we're called to do, we must put aside what we believe to be our own rights. We must deny a selfish desire for something we think we deserve in exchange for the good that someone else may or may not deserve. Paul charged Christians, "No one should seek their own good, but the good of others" (1 Cor. 10:24). This "others first" mentality does not come naturally. While children have to be taught to share and be kind and considerate to others, they do not have to be taught to be selfish. They can master that with no training at all. It just comes naturally. An example of this came on the heels of a trying shopping day.

It had been one of those days. It seemed that the errands would never end. I had started at one end of town and was slowly working my way home. Tired after a long day of zipping from Wal-Mart to the grocery store to the bank to the post office, I had become frustrated with my travel companions. My daughter Alex (who was five at the time), and her friend, Molly, were driving me batty with their endless arguments. As we approached the car one last time, I prepared myself to handle the conflict that I had avoided each time the girls entered the car—who got to climb in first.

I opened the back door and, once again, the girls pushed their way past my legs to see who could be the first one in. Before I could offer my wise counsel for finally resolving the conflict, Alex spoke up, "Molly, this time I am going to be kind and generous." I glanced down at her sincere little face and thought, *Praise the Lord! Maybe all those lectures about putting others first are finally beginning to sink in!* Thinking she was about to offer her friend the high honor of entering the car first, I waited patiently, anticipating the parental victory. Then she continued, "This time I am going to get in first because I want to be kind." Four-year-old Molly looked puzzled. With a scrunched up nose and raised upper lip she asked, "Huh?" As Alex dove in ahead of Molly she replied, "Molly, don't you know that the first will be last? And I don't want you to be last so I'm getting in first!"

This is manipulation at its finest. The amazing mind of a female is not something to be trifled with. Alex may have had her Scripture down, but the motive of her heart was definitely questionable.

One attitude that encourages selfishness is the deep need to protect "our rights." If we don't protect our own rights, who will? Trusting God to make sure our rights aren't violated is too risky, so we devote ourselves to the task.

Every year our extended family looks forward to a vacation in Big Sky, Montana. There's nothing like all eleven of us piling into a two-bedroom condo, skiing the snowy slopes all day, and then playing dominos by the cozy fire at night while eating junk food. It's the most wonderful time of the year for us, but it is also important for us to arrive home in a timely manner to accommodate our work schedules.

One year on the return trip we frantically ran through the airport with car seats, too much carry-on luggage, and two children under the age of five in tow. It was then that we were casually told by a rude flight attendant that our connecting flight had been canceled and there would be an overnight layover. No apologies, no compensation, no nothing. The more we talked about it, the more we decided that our rights had been violated. We had booked the flight in advance and paid far more than we should have for the tickets. We had a right to be flown home on the scheduled date, not twenty-four hours later. We held up our end of the bargain only to be flippantly dismissed with not so much as an apology. Well, no siree! I don't think so.

As the ringleaders in getting the others riled up, my brother Steven and I decided we would take control and handle the situation with a firm hand. We pranced to the manager's desk and demanded compensation. The manager listened as we clearly pointed out how our rights had been violated. Then he complied with our demands. Satisfied with the offer and quite proud of ourselves for successfully defending the rights of our deserving family, we strutted back to where the other family members sat, ready to share the spoils of victory. We had vouchers for transportation, hotel rooms, and meals. Everyone's spirit lifted.

Seated at the hotel restaurant, we were pleasantly surprised by the extended menu. We were even more surprised when I counted a generous $300 in meal vouchers, compliments of the airline. The flight would leave too early in the morning for breakfast, so we could only use them for the evening meal. Why not feast? After all, the airline had canceled our flight. They owed us. We *deserved* these vouchers, and we would milk the compensation for all it was worth. We ordered a generous variety of appetizers, steaks and potatoes, Greek and Caesar salads, shrimp and lobster bisque, and an assortment of bread. Then we wrapped things up with coffee and desserts galore. If we didn't max ourselves out with the sin of greed, we made up for it with the sin of gluttony. It was a gross indulgence to satisfy our "rights."

Once everyone was full and happy, the exhausted waitress slapped the bill on the table with a sigh of relief mixed with a bit of disgust.

My brother and I grinned with pride as we slapped the vouchers back at her, savoring the victory for which we had fought. Family members looked at us with admiration and appreciation for all that we had done on their behalf. We were heroes.

A few minutes later the waitress came back and smugly pointed out the small print at the bottom of each voucher. In all our gloating, we had missed the fact that the vouchers were designated for breakfast, lunch, and dinner, allotting a scarce per-person amount. Steven's face went white. Chocolate dripped from my chin. We had gone from heroes to complete idiots in mere seconds. I'm not even going to tell you the amount we had to fork out. Lesson learned: you get what you deserve.

Perhaps the worst part of the selfish way we responded was the impact for Christ we could have had on the waitress. Assuming she was not a believer, I wonder what went through her head as she watched us pray before avenging ourselves with food. And what about the airline manager? He had been bombarded with angry people demanding compensation for the overnight layover. He could have encountered the grace and kindness of God through the attitudes of my brother and me. Instead, he encountered a couple of hotheaded Christian jerks.

It's so easy to get caught up in "our rights" as an excuse not to serve others. While driving, do you ever inch your way forward and pretend not to see the car trying to merge into traffic? After all, you do have the right of way. Do you ever stand in line at the grocery store with a full shopping cart and dismiss the thought of offering to let the lady behind you with only two items go first? After all, it is your rightful place in line. Do you ever drive into a restaurant parking lot about the same time as someone else and rush to park so you can get in and be seated before them? After all, if you get there first, it's your right to be seated first. Do you ever feel your temperature rise when someone cuts in front of you in line? Why shouldn't that anger you? It's a blatant violation of your rights. Putting others first is not something that comes naturally, but it is something that brings glory and honor to Christ.

Another common hindrance to being focused on others is self-pity, a close relative to the martyr mentality. Many of us indulge in this practice far more than we realize. I must admit, I've thrown my share of pity parties. On many occasions I've tried to save face by wrapping myself in the cocoon of self-pity.

The root of self-pity is selfishness. How can there be self-pity without the consideration of self? Think about it. Who is exalted to guest of honor at a pity party? In order to pity myself, I have to be the focus. Rather than take responsibility and ownership for my failures or mistakes through humility, confession, and repentance, I indulge in a prideful form of false humility. I say, "I'm a nobody. I'm always messing up. Everyone would be better off without me. Woe is me. Me, me, me."

We often prefer self-pity to the gospel because of the subtle pleasure we receive from it. There is something very seductive about placing ourselves in a victim-martyr status, so we indulge in the gratification. Yet beyond the smoke and mirrors of self-pity is a profound self-righteousness and sense of entitlement. The only way to victimize ourselves is to believe that God has not been good to us. The self-pitying victim believes that life is not fair and that she has been shortchanged of something to which she is entitled. We cannot have self-pity and the gospel. Like oil and water, they do not mix. We can have one or the other, but not both.

Ironically, indulging in self-pity does not bring fulfillment. We were not created to seek the fulfillment of our own needs and wants, but to glorify the Father by doing his will. It is written in 2 Corinthians 5:15, "And [Jesus] died for all, that those who live should no longer live for themselves but for him who died for them and was raised again." His will is for us to show his love by denying self and seeking to serve others in his name. Surrendering and serving God brings fulfillment because it is the purpose of our creation.

It is impossible to live in self-pity while focusing on someone else. This is why Christ calls Christians to deny self and to live for his glory. When we are fully tuned in to Christ, and in turn other people, we take ourselves completely out of the equation. Our lives are no longer our own. We no longer consider what is best for us because "us" is no longer a part of our thoughts. By dying to ourselves we remove ourselves from needing to be right, preserving self, and craving respect and approval. There is no one left to feel sorry for and no one with whom to indulge in a pity party. That person died and has been raised up to a new life in Christ.

Paul was a man who practiced what he preached: specifically looking to the interests of others. Before Paul surrendered his life to Christ, he was a man of high standing and great influence. However, once he encountered Jesus and took hold of the love of God, the highest title he gave himself was "servant." When Paul began writing the book of Romans, he had to identify himself. There were many titles he could have used to describe himself. Paul was a man of impressive credentials, but all of his fancy titles and good standing among his peers meant nothing to him. Instead, he counted it an honor to be known as a servant of Jesus Christ. The words Paul penned about himself were, "Paul, a servant of Christ Jesus, called to be an apostle and set apart for the gospel of God" (Rom. 1:1). He even went so far as to call himself a slave to others. "Though I am free and belong to no man, I make myself a slave to everyone, to win as many as possible" (1 Cor. 9:19).

Of course, Jesus is our ultimate example of serving and putting others above ourselves. From washing the feet of his disciples to dying on the cross for our sins, Jesus served. If Jesus, who is the King of kings, took on the very nature of a servant and made himself nothing, surely we can follow his example by demonstrating simple acts of "otherness." The interesting thing is that when we put others above ourselves, not only is God glorified, but he also confirms his pleasure by bringing a surge of joy to our hearts. Jesus says that obedience to his commands brings joy: "I have told you this so that my joy may be in you and that your joy may be complete" (John 15:11).

Paul summed up true Christianity in Galatians 2:20: "I no longer live, but Christ lives in me." As Christians we are now unified with Christ, who has removed our selfishness and made us like him. He has set the example for a servant's heart—a heart like his. As his children we are meant to follow his example. Peter encouraged, "To this you were called, because Christ suffered for you, leaving you an example, that you should follow in his steps" (1 Peter 2:21).

7

The Religious Serial Sinner

and the Real Grace of God

Years ago, the media released ugly details concerning the fall of a prominent Christian leader. In addition to being a husband and father, the pastor of a 14,000-member church, and the president of a Christian organization with more than 30 million followers, he was well known for his views against homosexuality. Angered by his hypocrisy, his homosexual massage therapist of three years blew the whistle on their secret rendezvous. However, it is not the sin this man committed, but my sinful reaction toward him that brings me deep shame.

It was Sunday morning. I smiled my way through the church foyer, meeting and greeting everyone I passed on the way to Sunday school, taught eighth graders about showing others the love and forgiveness of Christ, sang and worshiped Jesus with teary eyes and a thankful heart, and soaked in a three-point sermon highlighting God's grace towards sinners. Life was good. We arrived home from church with my extended family, gathered around the table, held hands, thanked God for sending his Son to die for our sins, and began to chat as we dug into the pork tenderloin and mashed potatoes with gravy.

"Wasn't that a good sermon?" my mom asked. "Yes," we all agreed between bites. "I sure enjoyed the worship songs Brother Tim chose," Daddy said. "Me, too," my son said, taking a swig of sweet tea.

Once my hunger was satisfied, I decided to bring up the juicy news for dessert. "Did you hear about so-and-so? I mean, it's not gossip if it's in the news, right? Can you believe that man? Parading around like Mr. Christian spokesperson against homosexuality in the limelight, while sneaking around and living a completely different life behind closed doors. Could there be anything more horrifyingly hypocritical? You know what I think? I think he deserves a slow and painful death!" Everyone was silent. You could have heard a pin drop. Then came the conviction of the Holy Spirit. Oh, the wicked hypocrisy of my heart!

I spoke of that poor, fallen child of God as if his sins were more wicked than my own. I viewed him as being less worthy of living, less worthy of Jesus than I. Even worse, I saw him through the eyes of a proud sinner, rather than through the eyes of the forgiving, compassionate God who lives within me. According to the Bible, that man is no less a Christian and no more a sinner than I am. "For all have sinned and fall short of the glory of God" (Rom. 3:23). My sin of judging him was just as hypocritical as his sin of participating in what he spoke against.

Do you know who Christ spoke against? Not the fallen, repentant sinner, but the religiously judgmental. Of the sinner who seeks forgiveness the Almighty said, "If you repent, I will restore you that you may serve me" (Jer. 15:19). But of those who judge others he said, "Do not judge, or you too will be judged. For in the same way you judge others, you will be judged, and with the measure you use, it will be measured to you" (Matt. 7:1-2). I don't know about you, but my judgmental measuring cup can be pretty deep at times. I have been known to scoop out hefty loads of condemnation from the sinful bin of my heart and dump them on my Christian brothers and sisters.

In recognizing my own ugly sinfulness regarding the fall of my Christian brother, I am all the more thankful for the grace and redemption that are mine in Christ Jesus. It is frightening to realize that, without that redemptive grace, God would judge me with the same measuring cup I've used.

Religious Serial Sinner: One who measures spiritual status by human performance (rather than the finality of the cross) and refuses to extend grace to sinners or acknowledge his or her own sinful capabilities.

The Real Grace of God

For everything real, there is typically a counterfeit. There is counterfeit money, counterfeit jewelry, and counterfeit china. There are counterfeit furs and antiques, toys, clothes, and a slew of items that others have attempted to copy. While there is nothing more real than Jesus Christ, there have been others who tried to copy his status. Many have claimed to be God, but there is only one whose name is above all names. He is "King of kings and Lord of lords" (1 Tim. 6:15). He is "the Alpha and the Omega, the First and the Last, the Beginning and the End" (Rev. 22:13). He was and is and is to come (Rev. 1:8). He is Jesus Christ, Savior of the world—the real thing.

Christ is drawn to people who are real—people who see themselves for who they are (sinners in need of a Savior) and see him for who he is (Savior of sinners). For example, Jesus was drawn to the adulterous woman. When she was caught red-handed in adultery, her accusers brought her before Jesus and the people, demanding that she be stoned. God saw the phoniness of the woman's accusers, who would deny that they were as sinful as she. With prideful chins held high, they paraded her around as a sinner who deserved to be stoned and announced themselves as the ones worthy to do the stoning. They were right about the first part, but wrong about the second. Jesus called them on it: "Let any one of you who is without sin be the first to throw a stone at her" (John 8:7). Of course, they all tucked tails and ran.

Meanwhile, the woman never denied she was a sinner. When they hurled their insults and accusations at her, she didn't defend herself. She was real. She saw herself as a sinner in need of a Savior, and Jesus was drawn to her realness. He did not condemn her. Instead, he instructed her to leave her life of sin and come under his wing of grace (John 8:11).

In another instance Jesus was drawn to Matthew, a lying, cheating tax collector. Why? Because Matthew was real. He acknowledged himself a sinner, repented, and followed Jesus. The self-righteous Pharisees didn't like it one bit when Jesus had dinner in Matthew's house. They saw themselves as being better than Matthew. Therefore, they thought Jesus should want to dine with them rather than slum with a sinner in a pagan home. Jesus set them straight in Matthew 9:12-13. He said, "It is not the healthy who need a doctor, but the sick." He explained to the Pharisees, "But go and learn what this means: 'I desire mercy, not sacrifice.' For I have not come to call the righteous, but sinners."

Unfortunately, they didn't know what Jesus meant. They couldn't see past their own righteousness. They didn't understand that in order for the doctor to make them well, they had to first admit to being sick. The Pharisees missed out on the goodness of God because of a judgmental attitude toward others and an unwillingness to take a real look into their own hearts.

Scripture reveals story after story of Jesus being drawn to sinners who acknowledged their need for him. David is referred to as a man after God's own heart, yet David took another man's wife into his bed, got her pregnant, then had her husband murdered to cover it up. However, when David cried out to God, confessing adultery and murder, God extended grace and rescued him from sin. The heroes in Scripture were all rescued by God. Moses was a murderer. Noah was a drunk. Rahab was a prostitute. Aaron was an idolater. Paul was a blasphemer and a murderer, and the list continues. While there are consequences for disobedience, God rescues those who are willing to take an honest look at their sins and seek forgiveness.

Although Jesus is drawn to those who are real, he is not drawn to those who are "religious." My friend Becky wears a T-shirt that reads, "Religion is against my relationship." I think Jesus would like that. He desires us to indulge in a real relationship with him, one that involves repentance and redemption, rather than religious rituals and rule following as ways to earn righteousness.

The Pharisees believed that abiding by the law was a substitute for real repentance. However, Jesus compared rule following and religious acts to "filthy rags" (Isa. 64:6). Therefore, there is nothing we can do to win his favor. Favor is won by the work of Christ on our behalf. It is not by our good deeds, but through his righteousness alone that our sins are atoned for. Paul confirms, "For it is by grace you have been saved, through faith—and this is not from yourselves, it is the gift of God—not by works, so that no one can boast" (Eph. 2:8-9).

Jesus said of the Pharisees, who believed their righteousness came through their own religious acts, "These people honor me with their lips, but their hearts are far from me. They worship me in vain; their teachings are merely human rules" (Matt. 15:8-9). Jesus labeled them as people who washed the outside of the cup while the inside was still unclean (Matt. 23:25-26).

Jesus often condemned the Pharisees for demonstrating outward acts of religion such as tithing, elaborate praying, and rebuking the sins of those around them in an attempt to appear righteous before others. He said, "Woe to you, teachers of the law and Pharisees, you hypocrites! You are like whitewashed tombs, which look beautiful on the outside but on the inside are full of the bones of the dead and everything unclean. In the same way, on the outside you appear to people as righteous but on the inside you are full of hypocrisy and wickedness" (Matt. 23:27-28).

Those verses arouse my anger at any person who participates in church activities and "religious" acts but does not show mercy and compassion to others. However, if I am really honest with myself, I will admit that I am like that person. How often have I pointed a finger at someone else's wrongdoing and allowed it to make me feel better about myself and my life? While talking out loud to God during a prayer meeting or with a friend, how many times have I been pleased with the flow of my well-worded prayer, wondering if others were impressed? How often have I figured out a way to mention during a conversation that I helped someone in need, in hopes that those listening might deem me generous? Too many times. *Oh Lord, thank you for taking this wicked heart and washing it clean. It is only by your sacrificial blood that I am forgiven and found guiltless.*

God Calls Christians to Be Real

Why are we so afraid of being real? I believe it is often because we fear what others might think. We want to be accepted. We want to be respected. We want to be admired and liked. We're afraid of what might happen if others knew what was really in our hearts.

Too often, we fear man more than we fear God. The simple truth is this: We are all sinners in desperate need of a Savior. Our hearts are filled with every kind of evil. Mark wrote, "For it is from within, out of a person's heart, that evil thoughts come—sexual immorality, theft, murder, adultery, greed, malice, deceit, lewdness, envy, slander, arrogance, and folly" (7:21-22)

Some of us read this verse and think, *God must be talking about someone else.* We admit, "Oh sure, I've been deceitful before. I mean, it doesn't happen that often, but I am capable of telling a small fib now and then. However, I would never commit theft." Here's another: "I'll admit that I've been guilty of a little slander. Sometimes when I'm with 'the girls' we fall into a little gossip. However, I would never commit murder." One more: "Well, I am a man, you know. I've occasionally had a lustful thought about a woman. However, out of love and respect for my wife, I would never commit adultery."

Note that the passage does not say, "For from within, out of *some* people's hearts come. . . ." My pastor cautions us never to say *never.* It's a prideful and dangerous thing to proclaim ourselves above committing a certain sin. As a matter of fact, to do so is to say that God's Word does not apply to us. John reminds us, "If we claim to be without sin, we deceive ourselves and the truth is not in us" (1 John 1:8). A few verses later, he goes on to say, "If we claim we have not sinned, we make him out to be a liar and his word is not in us" (v. 10).

We are all capable of every kind of evil. I may say to myself, *I am not capable of murder.* However, if a man abducted my ten-year-old daughter and raped, tortured, and killed her, and I was alone with him with a loaded gun in my hand, I believe I would be capable of murder. If I had grown up being molested and beaten by a man and then became a victim of human trafficking, I could easily develop fear and hatred toward men. If I never felt loved or respected by the men in my life, but a compassionate, understanding, homosexual woman made me feel safe and loved, I believe I would be capable of falling into homosexuality.

I realize I am on dangerous ground here. I am not saying that circumstances excuse sinful behavior. I *am* saying that, given the right set of circumstances, we are capable of all kinds of evil, and we must admit this truth in order to be in agreement with the Word of God. The apostle Paul said, "No temptation has overtaken you except what is common to mankind" (1 Cor. 10:13). In other words, there is no temptation or capability for evil to which the human heart is immune. Satan is clever. He knows how to capitalize on circumstances, situations, and personal weaknesses. The Enemy may not seize opportunities to lure you with certain sins, but according to the Scripture, the potential to commit every sin is within every heart.

The second part of what Paul said in the same verse is the good news. "And God is faithful; he will not let you be tempted beyond what you can bear. But when you are tempted, he will also provide a way out so that you can endure it." Our way out is found in our identity in Christ. If we belong to Christ, he has overcome all of these temptations for us through his death, burial, and resurrection. Praise his name! Christ has covered our unrighteousness. "For Christ also suffered once for sins, the righteous for the unrighteous, to bring you to God" (1 Peter 3:18).

As Christians, we are no longer slaves to sin. Paul explained that since Christ died for us, we should "count [our]selves dead to sin but alive to God in Christ Jesus" (Rom. 6:11). We have been brought from death to life, and we are no longer given over to sin, but to God as instruments of righteousness (v. 13). We are not to continue living in sin as though God's grace was nothing more than insurance for forgiveness. Paul adds, "You have been set free from sin and have become slaves to righteousness" (v. 18).

The more we understand that our sins are covered by grace, the more we desire to live out of that grace. Some behave as though grace is an excuse to live out of our fleshly desires. "I can do anything I feel like because Christ forgives sinners," we say. How backward this sort of thinking is! It is because of his amazing grace that we no longer live in the flesh! The Bible says, "What shall we say, then? Shall we go on sinning so that grace may increase?" In other words, should we take advantage of God's grace by continuing in sin? "By no means!" the Bible says. "We are those who have died to sin; how can we live in it any longer?" (Rom. 6:1-2).

God actually invites us to take advantage of his grace—in a manner that far outweighs a shallow life of continued sin. He invites us to *live* in his grace, absorbing it to cover our old selves (before salvation) and saturating our new selves (after salvation) with his righteousness. If we truly understand that soaking in God's grace involves death and rebirth, we can only take advantage of it by living in it. In order to understand that Christ has won the victory, we have to first acknowledge that we are sinners, capable of the worst deeds imaginable, and then accept that we are dead to those capabilities only through our new life in Jesus. For we have been "crucified with Christ and we no longer live, but Christ lives in us. The life we live in the body, we live by faith in the Son of God, who loved us and gave himself for us" (Gal. 2:20, adapted). Praise his name! We are guiltless! He has won the victory for us! After we acknowledge and accept these truths, then we can fully rejoice with Paul's words, "'Death has been swallowed up in victory' . . . thanks be to God! He gives us the victory through our Lord Jesus Christ" (1 Cor. 15:54, 57).

Hope for the Serial Sinner

What does the term serial sinner *mean to you* after reading
this book? The outward manifestations of impatience, pride, selfishness, and self-righteousness are merely the fruit of a sinful heart.
Therefore, it is sin that causes us to behave the way we do. Because
we all demonstrate sin over and over in some form or fashion, we
are all serial sinners. But there is good news for serial sinners!

Throughout this book I have exposed hidden sins, exalted the
righteousness of Christ, and explained the commands of holiness
that God gives his children. Then I turned right around and stated
that, as sinners, we simply are incapable of keeping the commands
of God. Does this mean we should throw up our hands in defeat
and accept that we will always be serial sinners? Yes and no. It is
true that no matter how hard we try, we cannot overcome our sinful
status. However, the good news is that while we are serial sinners,
we are covered by the grace of God. Rather than viewing ourselves
as serial sinners, perhaps a more appropriate title in accordance
with the good news of the gospel would be *sinning saints*. We are
sinners, transformed into saints through the atonement of Christ.
Sound better? Yes, I thought so too!

Jesus has already won the victory and defeated sin on our behalf.
The work has already been done. All that is left for us to do is take
hold of victory over sin through Christ. I realize this is easier said
than done. After all, while we have been forgiven of sins and made
new, we still battle remaining sin, which ignites unholy thoughts and
actions. The pull of sin competes with the supremacy of God in our

hearts. This is why we must purpose to live in the power of Christ, not in our own power. Our hope lies in Christ.

There are misconceptions as to what it means to "live in Christ" among Christians. We often hear statements such as, "I gave that area of my life to God," or "I am surrendering this part of my life to the Lordship of Christ." This mentality is troublesome. It implies that our lives are to be parceled out like tracts of real estate to give to God as we see fit. If we take apart these statements to evaluate what is really being said, we find that they are based on efforts from the natural self, which leads to the slippery slope of self-reliance. When we rely on efforts from the natural self, our successes and failures become the measuring stick of our worth, which flies in the face of God's grace.

Lesley serves as one example. She "gave her cigarettes to God" during the weekend, but she reluctantly accepted one from her co-worker during lunch break on Monday. Lesley now feels like a failure as a Christian. Does God love Lesley less because she slipped and "took back" what she gave to God? Certainly not.

John, a recovering alcoholic, recently celebrated a successful year of abstinence. Now John feels that he meets one more qualification toward becoming a good Christian. Does God love John more now than he did a year ago when John was still struggling? Certainly not.

If good works do not win us favor with God, then it stands to reason that the sins that trip us up do not remove us from his favor. The more we understand the fullness of this grace-based love and acceptance, and the more we rest and invest at Calvary's cross, the more we experience guiltless living.

Giving up areas of our lives through the efforts of the natural self is merely slapping on a coat of Christian paint. As storms and different seasons of weather set in, it fades, cracks, and peels off. All our hard work is stripped bare, leaving us naked, vulnerable, and miserable. However, when we completely immerse ourselves in the blood of Christ, the stain of his love and grace soaks us. It is not a paint laid on the surface, but a permanent stain that nothing can penetrate.

Richard J. Foster writes, "The contrast between God's way of doing things and our way is never more acute than in this area of human change and transformation. We focus on specific actions; God focuses on us. We work from the outside in; God works from the inside out. We try; God transforms."[5]

Trying to give a particular area of our lives to God leads to self-assessments and pride in the natural self. The natural self should not be the starting point of our faith. The new life begins with dying to the natural self and burying attempts at righteousness. Whether we view them as failed attempts, which tend to leave us feeling defeated, or successful attempts, which tend to leave us feeling proud, is not what matters. What matters is that we let go—in the power of the Spirit—of the natural self completely and take hold of the new self, which is empowered through the death and resurrection of Christ. The truest sense of grace involves a full exchange of ashes for beauty. God does not want areas of our lives. He wants *our lives*.

There is no power in our own attempts to live right. We can determine to never be impatient or selfish or controlling, but without the power of the Holy Spirit working in and through us, we simply cannot achieve righteous living. We need to understand that the question is not "How can I live a righteous life without sinning?" The question is "How can I live more fully in Christ so that his righteousness comes forth in my life?" The battle over sin cannot be won by sheer willpower or by teeth-gritting determination. It is won by tucking ourselves underneath the full armor of God and trusting that God is not only fighting for us, he has already won the battle.

All that we need to overcome sin has been provided for us. The cure for sin is in the cross. Only through the power of Christ can sin's call be resisted. When we set our attention on the power of the sacrificial atoning work of Christ, our hearts become filled with his love for us and our love for him. Sin is crucified. It weakens, becomes unattractive, and eventually loses its pull. It's not that we focus on not sinning so much as it is that we focus on the glory and grace of God. As our hearts become more filled with God, there is less and less room for sin.

I have wondered why some people don't seem to struggle with sin as much as I do. I think, *Why is this such a temptation for me when it doesn't seem to tempt so-and-so at all? Why can't God just answer my prayer and take away my desire for sin? I pray that sin would not reign in my life, and that's really the desire of my heart, so why can't God just zap me and make the urge to sin go away?* Well, he did zap sin. He zapped it at Calvary. He invites me to enjoy the victory he has won for me and to dwell with him and rest in his righteousness.

The response he asks of me is to rely on him, to exist in him, meditate on him, and live in his amazing love. The more we pursue him, the closer we get to him. The closer we get to him, the more we delight in him. The more we delight in him, the less we delight in the things of this world, which pull us away and entice us to sin. The resisting of sin is found by residing in Christ.

As we set our affections on Jesus, his love weakens sin's lure. What once seemed irresistible becomes undesirable. The more we commit ourselves to ponder him, worship him, praise him, and talk with him, we will become so full of him that his character oozes from every pore.

Dear friend, I encourage you to experience real joy by asking Christ to enable you to dwell in the light of his glory and grace. Meditate on the wonders of the cross and the Savior who died and rose again for sinners to have life and victory. As attention transfers from self to God, the pull of sin will lose its attraction and die. I implore you to commit yourself to live where the empowerment of Calvary is greater than the enticement of sin. However, when you do sin, and you surely will, do not go about beating yourself up. The finality of the cross atoned for all of your sins—past, present, and future. Because of Christ's glorious work at Calvary, you can truly experience the full joy of *guiltless living*.

Bible Study Guide

CHAPTER 1

Critical/Encouraging

1. Read 2 Corinthians 10:5 and answer the following questions:

   a. As we rely on Christ to help us, what must we do to overcome a critical attitude?

   b. What is the difference between ignoring a critical thought and "making it obedient to Christ"?

   c. Think of a time when you made a critical thought obedient to Christ rather than pondering or voicing it. What might have happened had you voiced it? What were the blessings of making it obedient to Christ?

2. Read Romans 8:5-8 and list the differences in a mind controlled by the sinful nature versus a mind controlled by the Spirit.

3. What do the following verses say about our speech?

   a. Proverbs 12:18

   b. Proverbs 13:2-3

   c. Matthew 12:35-36

4. In Luke 18:9-14 Jesus told a parable about a Pharisee who used criticism as a way to make himself look good. What did Jesus say would happen to this man in the end?

5. Read Proverbs 15:28 and answer the following questions:

   a. In one sentence, explain how you have failed to obey this verse.

   b. How does one "weigh" an answer?

   c. Under what circumstances are you most likely to "gush evil" with your mouth?

    d. Ask God to show you two specific ways that you can practice this verse this week. Pray for his power to prompt and enable you during opportune moments.

6. What does Hebrews 3:13 reveal could happen if we fail to give and receive encouragement?

7. Describe a tough time in your life where Romans 8:28 applied.

8. Read Hebrews 10:25.

    a. What excuses do people today give for not meeting together?
    b. What is the purpose of meeting together as believers?
    c. Why does this verse stress that it is becoming more and more important to meet together?

9. Having a critical attitude shows a lack of trust and joy in the Lord. How do the following verses confirm this statement?

    a. Romans 8:18
    b. 2 Corinthians 12:9
    c. Philippians 4:4
    d. 1 Thessalonians 5:18
    e. James 1:2

10. What new truth has God revealed to you about being critical versus being encouraging? Write a prayer thanking him for the work of the Holy Spirit in your life.

CHAPTER 2

Proud /Humble

1. Through the power of Christ alone, God makes us more like him by convicting us of sin and calling us to return to him through repentance and forgiveness. Read 2 Chronicles 7:14 and answer the following questions:

   a. What four conditions does God set forth for a repentant Christian?

   b. What three promises will God fulfill for a repentant Christian?

2. It may seem that proud people go unpunished at times, but according to Isaiah 2:11-12 what will eventually happen to everyone who is proud?

3. During Saul's reign as king of Israel, he disobeyed God. When confronted with his sins, he demonstrated pride by defending himself and trying to cover up his true motives with justifications. What was the consequence of Saul's pride? (See 1 Samuel 13:14; 15:28.)

4. David became king of Israel after Saul's downfall. By comparison, David was guilty of sins far worse (in our eyes) than Saul. David was an adulterer and a murderer. Read David's repentant confession in Psalm 51.

   a. Why do you think Saul was condemned by God, but David was referred to as "a man after God's own heart"?

   b. Is there anything we can "do" to win back God's favor when we have sinned (51:16)?

   c. God did not require religious acts of sacrifice in order to forgive David his sins. What did God require (51:17)?

5. Jesus was drawn to outrageous yet humble and repentant sinners, not those who looked like perfect saints on the outside but

were full of pride on the inside. Apart from the atonement of Christ, the sin of pride would reign in all of our hearts, but Jesus took our pride to the cross and gave us his humility. What a gracious God we serve! What do the following verses say about pride and humility?

a. Proverbs 16:5
b. Proverbs 18:12
c. Obadiah 1:3
d. Luke 14:11
e. James 4:10

6. Look up Mark 10:43-44. What did Jesus say about those who want to be great and first?

7. In understanding God's greatness we are humbled. What was Job's response when God revealed his greatness?

a. Job 40:4
b. Job 42:5-6

8. Read Isaiah 57:15 and answer the following questions:

a. What do you think it means to be contrite and lowly in spirit?
b. How does God respond to a person who, by his power, walks in humility?

9. What are some ways that pride might affect our relationships with other people?

10. While reading this chapter and studying God's Word, has the Holy Spirit revealed any hidden pride in your heart? If so, write a prayer confessing areas of pride in your life and asking God to help you walk in humility.

CHAPTER **3**

Controlling/Sovereign

1. Explain how the sovereignty of Christ is revealed in the following passages:

    a. Matthew 8:28-34

    b. John 21:1-6

2. Read John's account of the death of Lazarus found in John 11:1-44 and then answer the following questions:

    a. When Jesus received word that Lazarus was sick, how did he respond? (11:4)

    b. According to Jesus, why was Lazarus facing sickness and death? (11:4)

    c. Why was Jesus glad he was not present when Lazarus died? (11:14-15)

    d. Jesus knew that Lazarus would be raised from the dead, yet he was "deeply moved in spirit and troubled" to the point that he actually wept (11:33-35). Why do you think Jesus demonstrated such emotion?

3. Read Matthew 8:23-27. Why do you think Jesus was able to sleep under such frightening circumstances?

4. When Peter realized that Jesus was walking on water, he wanted to do the same. How did trust play a part in Peter's ability to walk on water? How did control play a part in his sinking (Matthew 14:22-31)?

5. Read 2 Peter 3:8 and answer the following questions:

    a. How does our concept of time differ from God's?

    b. If we viewed time from an eternal perspective, how might that affect our reactions to trials and heartaches?

6. We often resist trusting God by trying to control people and situ-

ations. Yet God is ultimately in control. What do the following verses tell us about God's control over all things?

   a. Matthew 28:18
   b. Luke 4:38-41
   c. John 10:17-18
   d. Colossians 1:17
   e. Colossians 1:18

7. Have you ever tried to control someone's opinion of you through manipulation, justification, or lying? What do the following verses say about wanting to win the approval of others?

   a. 1 Samuel 16:7
   b. Luke 16:15

8. What do the following verses say about trusting God?

   a. Psalm 56:4
   b. Psalm 111:7
   c. Psalm 112:7
   d. Isaiah 26:3

9. Consider something (or someone) in your life that you struggle to control.

   a. What are you afraid will happen if you release control?
   b. How does this fear line up with the Word of God?
   c. How has fighting for control affected your emotions or level of anxiety?
   d. In evaluating your answers to a, b, and c, is it possible that your efforts to control this person or situation have become an idol in your life?
   e. Control is often the result of fear or selfishness, both of which Christ has overcome for us through his death and resurrection. Through his provision, we can lay these things down and have his peace and rest. Are you willing to live in the power of Christ, trusting him to enable you to let go of control?

10. Write your own prayer based on Psalm 139:23-24.

CHAPTER **4**

Impatient/ Patient

1. For 400 years, the Israelites were enslaved to the Egyptians. God brought plagues on Egypt, forcing Pharaoh to release the Israelites from captivity. Read about the events that took place shortly after their release in Exodus 14:10-31.

   a. How did the Israelites feel when they were trapped between the Red Sea and the approaching Egyptian army (14:10)?

   b. How did Moses respond to the fear of his people (14:13)?

   c. God wants his people to trust him for salvation, whether it's spiritual salvation or physical salvation. Often in times of trouble we tend to cast blame or fight for control. Moses assured the people that God would fight for them. What instructions pertaining to their physical salvation did Moses give the blame-shifting Israelites (14:14)?

   d. How do these same instructions apply to our spiritual salvation (Eph. 2:8-9)?

   e. What was God's purpose in rescuing the Israelites (Ex. 14:17-18)?

2. The Israelites had a hard time "being still" and "waiting on God." Think of a time when you took matters into your own hands rather than patiently waiting on God.

   a. What were the results?

   b. How might things have turned out better had you waited?

3. What do the following verses tell us about the patience of God?

   a. Nehemiah 9:17

   b. Nahum 1:3

   c. 2 Peter 3:15

4. According to Ecclesiastes 7:8, what is patience better than?

5. As we trust Jesus to demonstrate his humility through us, he is

glorified. Look up Philippians 2:3-4. What specific instructions are given to Christians for imitating Christ's humility?

6. Consider a time when you demonstrated pride rather than patience.

   a. What were the results?

   b. If you could go back and depend on God to work through you to demonstrate patience rather than pride, in what ways might the situation have turned out differently?

7. Perhaps one of the hardest times to hold on to patience is when someone has wronged us. What does the Bible say about patience in this situation?

   a. Psalm 37:7
   b. Proverbs 14:29
   c. Proverbs 15:18
   d. Proverbs 19:11

8. In what situation do you find yourself most impatient? Are you most impatient when dealing with certain people, such as your children, your spouse or your coworkers? Or are you most impatient when you are running late for an event, under a lot of pressure or in a stressful situation?

9. No matter what triggers your impatience, God has already provided his patience to be lived out through you. As you depend on his patience to work through you, in what specific ways might your responses to people or situations differ?

10. Write a prayer asking God to live his patience through you so that others might be blessed for his glory.

CHAPTER 5

Miserly/Generous

1. God is generous in answering our prayers in accordance with his will. What do the following verses say about God's generosity?

    a. Psalm 65:5
    b. Matthew 7:7-8
    c. Acts 2:21

2. If God said to you, "Ask for whatever you want and I'll give it to you," what would you ask for? God asked King Solomon that very question. Read 1 Kings 3:5-14 to find out what took place.

    a. What statement made by Solomon demonstrated a heart of humility (3:7)?
    b. What did Solomon ask for (3:9)?
    c. God was pleased that Solomon's requests were not selfish in nature. What might Solomon have asked for that would have been selfish in nature (3:11)?

3. God was generous in answering Solomon's prayer. How did God grant even more than Solomon asked (1 Kings 3:12-13)?

4. What did God demand of Solomon as a prerequisite for granting him a long life (1 Kings 3:14)?

5. The beauty of God calling us to walk in his ways and obey his commands is that we can only do those things through his power in us. The more we experience his power working in and through us, the more our lives are filled with the reality and joy of his glorious presence. It just doesn't get any better than that! As we walk in his ways through the power of his Spirit, he has our best interests at heart. How do these verses confirm this truth?

    a. Deuteronomy 6:3
    b. Jeremiah 29:11
    c. John 15:10-11

6. What does God's Word say about the blessings that come from being generous?

   a. Proverbs 11:25
   b. 2 Corinthians 9:6

7. While God commands us to be generous, we are not capable of obeying this command. What do the following verses say about the source that enables us?

   a. 2 Corinthians 9:8-11
   b. Galatians 2:20-21
   c. Philippians 1:6

8. Read Matthew 6:1-4 and answer these questions.

   a. Is it possible to have a sinful motive for being generous?
   b. What are some ways we might seek recognition for generosity?
   c. What does God say happens when we seek a pat on the back for a generous act?
   d. How can we avoid prideful giving?

9. Acts 20:35 says, "It is more blessed to give than to receive." Write about a time when you were blessed by giving.

10. 10. Write your own prayer based on Paul's words in 1 Timothy 1:12-17.

CHAPTER **6**

Selfish/Serving

1. Christ empowers us to serve with a motive of "otherness" rather than for personal gain or recognition. Read the parable of the lost son in Luke 15:11-32.

   a. How did the father respond to his repentant son (15:22-24)?
   b. How did the older brother respond (15:28)?
   c. What comparisons did the older son make between himself and his younger brother (15:29-30)?
   d. What does the response of the older brother reveal about his motive for serving?
   e. Have you ever served for the glory of recognition? Explain.
   f. Christ has covered our sinful motives through his work at Calvary. However, when we live out of our sin nature instead of being dependent on the finished work of Christ, we wind up serving with wrong motives. According to Philippians 4:6-7, how does prayer play a part as God helps us to overcome our sin nature?

2. How do you respond when others are recognized or honored? Are you happy for them or do you feel you are not receiving the credit you deserve? How does your attitude line up with what you have learned about having a servant's heart and putting others above yourself?

3. Christ became man to fulfill the Father's will and to atone for our sins through his death and resurrection. According to the following verses, what other purpose did his humanity serve?

   a. Hebrews 2:18
   b. 1 Peter 2:21

4. Selfishness is the opposite of love in many ways. List the descriptions of love according to 1 Corinthians 13:4-7.

    a. Love is not:

    b. Love is:

5. What do the following verses tell us about loving and serving others?

    a. Romans 12:10

    b. Romans 15:1-3

    c. Galatians 5:14

    d. 1 John 3:16

6. Look up Philippians 2:4. Is there an area in your life where you are looking to your own interests rather than the interests of others? Pray about specific ways you could actively look to the interests of others and ask God to empower you to obey him in these areas.

7. In Ruth 1, we learn about Naomi losing her husband and two sons. Although it would mean facing life alone, Naomi urged both of her daughters-in-law to leave her in order that they might remarry.

    a. How did Orpah respond, and what did this reveal about her desire to serve by placing others (namely her mother-in-law) above herself (1:14)?

    b. How did Ruth respond, and what did this reveal about her desire to serve and place others above herself (1:15-17)?

8. When the teachers of the law asked Jesus which was the most important commandment, what two-fold answer did Jesus give? See Mark 12:28-31.

9. Read the parable of the good Samaritan in Luke 10:25-37.

    a. What unselfish feeling did the Samaritan have for the man who had been beaten and robbed (10:33)?

    b. List all of the ways the Good Samaritan served the helpless man (10:34-35).

    c. Can you recall a specific time when God called and equipped you to serve someone in need with your time, money, or an act of kindness? Record what happened.

10. God has gifted us all to serve in different ways. Read 1 Peter 4:10-11 and answer the following questions:

a. For what purpose do we use our gifts?

b. From whom does our strength to serve come?

c. Write a few sentences to explain how God is glorified through our acts of service, specifically impacting the lives of non-Christians.

CHAPTER 7

Religious/Real

1. Read Matthew 15:1-20.

   a. What law/tradition did the Pharisees accuse the disciples of breaking? (15:2)

   b. What command of God did Jesus accuse the Pharisees of breaking for the sake of their tradition? (15:3-6)

2. List some man-made expectations the church puts on Christians. Do you feel like a "bad Christian" when you fail to meet the church's expectations? Why?

3. Consider your answer to the previous question. Compare your feelings to the truth of God's Word:

   a. Proverbs 29:25

   b. Isaiah 51:7

   c. 1 Corinthians 10:31

   d. Galatians 1:10

   e. 1 Thessalonians 2:4

4. The tradition of the Pharisees was to withhold money from their elderly parents in order to use it as a gift devoted to God. What was their real motive? (See Matthew 6:2.)

5. Read Matthew 6:16-18 and answer the following questions:

   a. What did the hypocrites do so that others would know they were fasting?

   b. What do you think Jesus meant when he said that they had received their reward in full?

   c. How do we express sincerity in fasting?

   d. Have you ever been guilty of doing something "religious" for the sake of impressing others? If so, how do you feel about that now?

6. Read Matthew 6:5-8 and list some of the differences in a "religious" prayer versus a "real" prayer.

7. What does Jesus say we should do before pointing out wrongs in a Christian brother or sister's life? (See Matthew 7:1-5.)

8. While Jesus commands us to tithe, what three things did he say were even more important? (See Matthew 23:23.)

9. Jesus rebuked the hypocritical Pharisees and teachers of the law in the "Seven Woes" listed in Matthew 23. Although they had sinned against God in every way, grace flowed from the heart of Christ as he shared his desire for them. Look up Matthew 23:37 and answer the following questions:

   a. What did Jesus long to do for these sinful people?
   b. Why did Jesus refrain from doing what he longed to do?

10. Write a prayer asking Jesus to reveal hidden sins. Be still before the Lord for a few minutes and allow the Holy Spirit to speak to your heart. Confess the sins that are brought to your attention, thank Jesus for atoning for your sins and ask for his help to live in the power of the gospel. To him be the glory!

Endnotes

1. *Webster's II New College Dictionary* (Boston, New York: Houghton Mifflin, 1999), 240.

2. Ginger Hubbard, *Don't Make Me Count to Three* (Wapwallopen, Pa.: Shepherd Press, 2003), 23-24.

3. "Road rage hits most drivers," BBC News, August 13, 2003, online at http://news.bbc.co.uk/2/hi/uk_news/3146781.stm. Last accessed November 30, 2008.

4. Newton Hightower, "The Startling Statistics on Road Rage," Bharat Bhasha, http://www.bharatbhasha.com/health.php/9705. Last accessed November 30, 2008.

5. Richard J. Foster and James Bryan Smith, *Devotional Classics* (New York: Harper One Publishing, 2005), 12.